Unexpected Inheritance

Unexpected Inheritance

To Linda!
Vest wishes
SM Vest
4-18-2015

Stephen M. Vest

BUTLER BOOKS

PHOTOS:

On front cover: Mamaw lived alone near Clearwater Beach, Florida, for more than 40 years. Here she poses on Honeymoon Island, near Dunedin. (Photo by Harold G. Vest)

On back cover: Little Stevie was quite the fashion plate as seen during an annual visit to Mamaw's first Florida home. (Photo by Harold G. Vest)

Opposite title page: Afternoon fishing trips were frequent during visits with Mamaw. Sometimes there were even some fish caught. (Photo by Harold G. Vest)

Designed by Eric Butler

ISBN 978-1-935497-97-4

Printed in the United States of America
First printing October 2014

Published by
Butler Books
P.O. Box 7311
Louisville, KY 40257
phone: (502) 897-9393
fax: (502) 897-9797
www.butlerbooks.com

Contents

"These people are . . . well, certainly worth writing about. Bless their pea-picking hearts."

—*Uncle Skeeter*

Photos of Dad were rare during the 1960s and '70s as he was generally behind the camera. This one with Little Stevie was taken at Clearwater Beach. (Photo by Margie Vest)

Mom and Little Stevie enjoy a free Coca-Cola at the
Georgia Welcome Center. (Photo by Harold G. Vest)

Epigraph

IN SOUTHERN LOUISIANA'S CAMERON PARISH stands a statue of a mother shielding her helpless young son from the onslaught of an approaching storm. Engraved with the plea "Do not harm my children," the statue pays homage to Hurricane Audrey, which killed more than 400 people and caused more than one billion dollars in damages in late June 1957.

Audrey struck a little more than four years before I was born.

CHAPTER I

Tag, You're It

I CAN CLEARLY PICTURE HIM heading north on Interstate 75, singing along with Keith Urban on the radio. His head is swaying back and forth to the rhythm as he passes the exits for Etowah, Athens, and Sweetwater.

> *And the sun is shining, this road keeps winding*
> *Through the prettiest country*
> *From Georgia to Tennessee.*

As he and his lady fair draw closer to home, somewhere in the foothill ridgelines of northeast Tennessee, he's still singing, only louder.

> *. . . And I got the one I love beside me*
> *My troubles behind me*
> *I'm alive and I'm free*
> *Who wouldn't want to be me?*

That was when his battered minivan first began to sputter and then to coast, and he limped into a Pilot gas station southwest of Knoxville, Tennessee.

What happened in the 90 minutes between his discovery that he, like Urban in the song, didn't *have any money in his pocket*, and his credit card—if he had one—was not going to work, and my arrival on the scene, I don't know.

I'm pretty sure I do not want to know.

As for me, I was en route home, alone, from a semiannual gathering of middle-aged regional magazine publishers at the Atlanta Airport Marriott. By the time I arrived at the bustling gas station, it was a clear Smoky Mountain evening with a lovely three-quarter moon. As I started pumping my gas, he approached me. His thin hands were pressed together in front of his chest in a prayerful pose as he bowed to me as if I were either a Tibetan monk or possibly a martial arts instructor.

He looked a mess. His shirt was tucked in, but too large for his frame, causing it to billow awkwardly around his cinched beltline. His belt was brown. His shoes were black.

On a good day, this twenty-something-year-old could have passed for Shaggy on *The Adventures of Scooby-Doo*, right down to his crusty, auburn-blond chin whiskers, but this obviously wasn't—at least anymore to him—a good day.

"Dear sir, would you be so kind as to spare any pocket change?"

Oh, good grief, I thought. Is this really what the world has come to? Just over there are the Mini Cooper and BMW dealers and here, not 300 yards away, we have methamphetamine addicts blatantly panhandling in the well-lit shadows of Knoxville's trendy Kingston Pike shops? Maybe, with that pose, he'd have better luck up the hill at the Wasabi Japanese Steakhouse.

"I'm sorry," I said, halfheartedly rooting around in a pocket of my khaki pants. "Look, I have a dime and a few pennies, and that's not going to do you much good."

As I gave him what I had, I noticed that dangling from his neck was a white laminated passkey identification card. The side containing his name and picture was toward his protruding ribs. Facing me was a barcode and the bold embossed black letters "I" and "T," which I assumed meant he had a challenging and rewarding career in the information technology field. I thought of making some witty comment about his tag saying "it,"—get it? tag, you're it?—but my eldest daughter Katy has told me repeatedly over the years that I should refrain from saying any old thing that pops into my silly old head, and I, for once, heeded her sage advice.

"Thank you, kind sir. I understand. It's just that me and the missus have been trapped here for more than an hour and a half, and we just want to get home," he said as he slunk, shoulders sagging, back to his overstuffed, tattered Chevy minivan.

As I climbed back into my wife's new, slightly used, Mercury Mariner with the automatic seat warmers, I pondered my dinner choices. In the interest of time, it needed to be something quick. Should I get a Number One with cheese (no onions, no tomatoes) from the Wendy's attached to the gas station or venture inside the Pilot food mart and spoil myself with a Hostess Suzy Q and a small carton of two-percent milk? Oh, the thought of the devil's food cake and the white creme filling was difficult to resist, but I held off the urge. "That is the way to madness," I told myself. "You know all too well, bucko, it is called devil's food for a reason."

Putting the Mariner into gear, I glanced to my left, and IT was slamming his fists on the cigarette- and snack-strewn dashboard and his head against the black steering wheel. I was pretty sure he was about to cry. The object of his desire, a rather hefty maiden, was splayed out across the front seat and spilled out of the open passenger door. Her pose, coupled with my present geographical location, conjured up memories of Lulu Roman, a regular on *Hee Haw*, except instead of fanning herself on a countrified television set, she was halfheartedly working a seek-and-find while chewing on a supersized Baby Ruth candy bar.

Ever aware of my own tendencies, at times, to be overly judgmental and outright condescending, my mind was suddenly flooded with images of my benevolent father, a big fan of *Hee Haw*, always helping others in need. Jumper cables at the ready, a spare gas can, a kind word were all a part of his ample arsenal. Dad was never reluctant in stepping forward—no matter how scruffy, no matter how fat. He would never have labeled a stranded traveler a meth addict when the obvious evidence pointed toward a penchant for sugary treats.

As I waited my turn in the Wendy's drive-thru, my mind wandered. I found myself in one of a half dozen Southern Baptist Sunday School classes Dad taught over the years. I could faintly hear the story of the Good Samaritan helping the injured man along the road from Jerusalem to Jericho, and Jesus's parable in the 25th chapter of Matthew, the 40th verse: "Verily I say unto you, inasmuch as ye have done it unto one of the least of these my brethren, ye have done it unto me."

While "IT" reminded me of Shaggy, there was, without question, something about him that reminded me of my high-school-aged son Christopher, too. It wasn't the scruffiness necessarily. Maybe it was his deeply set hazel eyes.

"I hope I never find myself in this situation," I mumbled to myself.

Then I remembered that I had been in this exact situation more than three decades ago and to lesser degrees numerous times over the years.

Slick Johnson, my own goatee-sporting high school friend, and I were on our way home from a cold, rainy weekend of camping at Rough River Lake when we ran out of gas on Dixie Highway in Muldraugh, Kentucky, a gritty north-bound commercial strip outside the fence line of Fort Knox that is every bit as lovely as its name. That brief stretch of "the Dixie," speckled with used car lots, pawn shops and 25-cent adult peep shows, is without doubt the closest reflection of the ancient road to Jericho that can be found in Kentucky.

Slick and I pushed my lime-green 1975 Mustang II into a weathered Convenient Food Mart gas station. Neither of us had any cash, other than a dime and a few pennies, and a sign on the front of the store proudly declared that it accepted "NO PERSONAL CHECKS, NO EXCEPTIONS."

For what seemed like several agonizing hours, maybe 90 minutes, we pleaded with the unsympathetic store clerk to spot me a dollar's worth of gas to get us down Muldraugh Hill into Jefferson County, a distance of five or six miles. If I could only get there, my overused ATM card would probably—if I weren't overdrawn again—work.

"Look," I said. "I'll leave my driver's license and wallet here with you. I'll go down the hill, get some money and come back here and fill up my car. I'll even let you keep the change."

"Nope," he said.

"Please?" I said.

"Nope is nope."

Never working up enough nerve to ask any of the other patrons for money, Slick and I eventually gave up and called Dad collect from the payphone in the parking lot. Dad, without the slightest hesitation, dutifully drove more than 30 miles from Louisville to help us. While it was inconvenient for Dad, it was humiliating for me.

"Do you think you should have planned your trip a little better?" Dad asked, politely.

"Yes, I know, Dad. I know."

In those days it couldn't have cost more than $10 to fill the Mustang II, a miniature, discounted version of the original Ford classic, but, with traffic, it cost Dad more than an hour and a half of his precious Sunday afternoon—time he could have been spending helping someone more grateful and deserving.

Busy sulking, I'm not sure I even thanked Dad before driving away.

That certainly wasn't the last time Dad would come to my aid, but with the exception of that one day in Muldraugh, whenever I've found myself in need, due to misfortune or my own poor planning, someone has always, like the Good Samaritan on the road to Jericho, attempted to help.

Verily I say . . .

"OK, OK," I said to myself, surprisingly loudly, as I accepted my white paper-sacked dinner from the Wendy's window.

I half hoped IT would have been helped during my five-minute journey around the multi-tasked building, but no, as I pulled forward, he was still there. I drove my wife's Mariner up to the pump next to IT's gray Chevy van. Through my still-open window I asked him how much gas he would need to get the rest of the way home. "Oh, no more than five dollars, kind sir," he said, sheepishly, with an expression of amazement, as if we had never met.

"Fine," I said. "I can certainly help with that."

Before you start thinking I'm a nice guy without reservations, I no sooner had pulled out my credit card from my bulging brown wallet than I feared this was all some form of elaborate scam, and IT—being that he worked in the information technology sector—was now going to somehow steal my precious identity to order who-knows-what from the darker side of the Internet. This kind deed, I knew, was going to come back and bite me. I just didn't know when or how.

Why, I thought, had IT selected me? Did I look like a soft touch, or was it that I looked well heeled in my new nine dollar and ninety-five cent blue-and-white-striped dress shirt, bought the day before at the Walmart in Williamsburg, Kentucky?

"How about 10?" I asked. "Are you sure that will get you home?"

"Oh, yeah," he said. "That'll be more than enough, kind sir."

"Do you want to pump the gas?" I asked.

"No," he said. "You should, if you don't mind."

IT paused.

He pressed his thin hands together and bowed to me again. He nervously fiddled with the lanyard to his name badge. Lulu hadn't uttered a word nor moved a muscle.

Then IT said, "I certainly wouldn't want you to think I was trying to take advantage of you—like the last guy did."

CHAPTER 2

Dad Lost

MY FATHER LITERALLY GAVE ME everything I ever asked for. In some small way, his ability to deliver was woven into my understanding of the universe. It was as fundamental as air for humans or water for fish. He may not have given those things I so badly wanted, whatever they were, in the manner I wished or expected, but he eventually delivered, without fail.

At the time of his death, the one request Dad hadn't fulfilled, the tidbit I wanted most, was a sense of history, his story, what made him tick, to pass on to my own children and my children's children. Sure, he'd told me the story about how he and his younger brother Charles drove their father's old Ford truck the 20 miles from the family farm to the county seat to take their driver's test. He told me how they—unexposed to need to know how to parallel park—both failed, then got back in the truck and drove back home.

It wasn't that Dad wouldn't talk. He chatted with almost everyone. He just wouldn't dwell on the past, and when it came to discussing himself, for the most part, he had little, if anything, to say. "Nobody wants to hear all that stuff," he would say. Or, "I don't understand what it is you want to know."

It wasn't that I didn't ask. I tried on many occasions to get him to open up. I had asked leading questions, going on what an attorney or journalist might call a fishing expedition, but he never took the bait.

There have numerous been times during writing workshops that I've felt a mild aggravation, a disappointment of sorts, with my father. After all, he's the one who encouraged me to take up this infernal trade. He's the one who brought home tablets of writing paper, legal pads and glossy black US Government ballpoint pens. He's the one who pilfered unclaimed reconditioned typewriters from his US Army Corps of Engineers office for me to use and gave me my first and second copies of Strunk & White's *The Elements of Style*. He read to me at night and introduced me to the writings of his favorite authors— Jack London, James Thurber, John Steinbeck.

What Dad didn't give me was the thing most writers have— the all-important abusive relationship, a gristmill of pain upon which to build my angst-filled career.

He didn't abandon me as a child.

He didn't beat my mother.

He didn't drink.

He didn't smoke.

He didn't cuss.

He didn't put undue pressure on me to fulfill his unmet dreams, whatever they may have been, and he didn't pile layers of guilt on me for my lack of success. He attended all my school programs and didn't miss a half inning of a single Little League baseball game. When, at 36, I decided to abandon my pursuit of the Pulitzer Prize, leave my moderately success- ful newspaper career, and launch a general-interest monthly magazine focused on our home state, Dad was the first to invest. He was the first to subscribe. When we needed to build circulation, he filled the trunk of his car with magazines and drove the interstates and back roads of Kentucky, from one end of the state to the other, giving them out at hotels, schools, hospitals, and doctors' offices. He was always there—supportive, always supportive.

How utterly thoughtless.

Writing certainly would be easier if Dad had put his cigarettes out on my forearms and the backs of my hands, but as I said, he didn't smoke. Going to counseling would be much less painful if I had someone other than myself on whom I could blame all my shortcomings.

In those moments when I am not the world's best father, which are frequent, it would be oh-so-convenient to be able to claim that it was because Dad hadn't set a good example, but no, I couldn't be so lucky. No underlying pain. No unresolved issues. No fodder upon which to build my inspired tale of woe. Dad apparently didn't know that when you neglect to leave your writer son some emotional baggage, you leave him nothing to fall back on. What possibly could he have been thinking?

* *

I once wrote a flattering magazine column about the demise of a friend's father to whom I had been marginally close. I wrote a glowing account of his storied life and times and the social significance of his passing, as it came during a time when veterans of World War II were dying at a rate of more than a thousand a day. Soon after, another friend's father passed away, and the son, my friend, asked me to write a similar tribute to his father. But I didn't know his father all that well, and I felt, at the time, I had nothing left to say about the loss of a father.

It would be less than a year before Dad died.

I asked Dad, given that father knows best, what I should do? "How can I write about someone whom I barely knew and make it sound sincere?"

"You can't," Dad said with a smirk. "You simply can't write about them all." He then paused, touched two fingers to his closely shaved chin as if he were pondering something important and said, "There are two universal truths about fathers: We all have them—good, bad or indifferent—and they all die."

* *

Dad's father Pops, a master carpenter and homebuilder, died a month to the day before I was born. In the rare stories I've heard about him, I learned that he fiddled in his small workshop nightly for decades, trying to create a perpetual-motion machine; he chain-smoked King Edward cigars; he sometimes listened to the Cincinnati Reds on his Crosley radio. I never heard anything disparaging about Pops. Not much good, either. In the annals of fatherhood, my guess is that Pops was one of those "indifferent" ones. I can't help but wonder how my own children will describe me, or not, when I'm gone. I can just hear them now: "He sometimes listened to the Cincinnati Reds on the car radio. And college basketball. He enjoyed telling jokes that no one else understood. He didn't smoke, but he enjoyed Oreos and Suzy Qs." It rightfully could be much worse. "He yelled a lot for no reason. He always promised to build me a playhouse in the backyard, but he never did."

* *

Dad was a blue-eyed blond, two traits he inherited from his mother. He was a member of "America's Greatest Generation," a World War II Navy veteran with more than a half-dozen battle stars. Dad was of average height, about five-foot-nine, and average weight, maybe 160 pounds. Other than his wispy hair, he was, at least in terms of style, typical of his generation in every way. As a younger man, he wore Old Spice, like his father and father-in-law. From its launch by Fabergé in 1964 (the year we moved to Ohio), Dad wore Brut, "the Essence of Man," marketed as representing traditional masculine strength of character.

When sideburns were commonplace, he had them. When everyone had a mustache, he did, too. His clothes closet contained plaid pants, white belts and white shoes. His ties, mostly gifts from his children and grandchildren, were a horrid montage of the 1950s,'60s and '70s.

Dad's story begins on September 9, 1921, near Waverly, Virginia, a small town on the northern edge of the Dismal Swamp, one hundred and ten thousand acres of forested wetlands that span parts of southeastern Virginia and north-eastern North Carolina. It was there that poet Robert Frost, as a spurned, angst-filled young man, thought of walking away from a rejected marriage proposal and losing himself in the swamp, never to be seen again.

Pops, a fifth-generation Kentuckian, had taken the family to Virginia, the land of his ancestors, to get in on the ground floor of an emerging lumber business that—at least for Pops—never materialized. Pops soon packed his family up and returned to northern Kentucky, where, for the rest of his life, he kept his family constantly moving.

Pops would buy a house and begin building another house nearby. He would then put both dwellings up for sale. Depending on which one sold first, Pops's family—which included Dad's older sister, Gladys; an older brother, Bill; and Charles, the baby—would either stay put and start work on another house, or move. By Dad's best count he had 22 different addresses before striking out on his own shortly after his 19th birthday.

Dad took work as a civilian surveyor for the US Army Corps of Engineers based out of Louisville, Kentucky, and traveled throughout the Midwest, living on the road in places such as New Harmony, Princeton and Evansville, Indiana, Carbondale and Mount Vernon, Illinois, and Madisonville and Paducah, Kentucky, until joining the US Navy with the outbreak of World War II.

"I chose the Navy because it seemed to be the cleanest branch of service," I overheard Dad tell one of the men in his Sunday School class. "But, you know, it certainly didn't take me long to figure out how they kept it so clean. There wasn't a spare moment when you didn't have either a mop or a paint brush in your hand."

Maybe it was all the childhood shuffling that made him adaptable and buoyant, but Dad never met a stranger. I can remember how, on our numerous vacation trips, mostly to Florida, he would come out of an interstate rest stop or Stuckey's restaurant with a new friend. "This is Joe," he would say. "He's from Toledo. His wife Ruth is a registered nurse, and his son Pete is going to Bowling Green State to become a horticulturist."

* *

Dad was the chairman of deacons in the Southern Baptist church, the Sunday School superintendent, and, in retirement, a member of Gideons International, the volunteer organization that places Bibles in hotel and motel rooms across America and in nearly 200 other countries. In his home church, Dad was always the first volunteer for the "visitation" committee, because he really enjoyed talking to people.

Jesus said: I will make you fishers of men.

The visitation committee met at seven o'clock on Tuesday evenings and went fishing—dropping in, often unannounced, at the homes of anyone who had recently visited the church, others who had not attended in some time, or those people (members or otherwise) whom fellow churchgoers suggested might be in need of a visit: the shut-ins, the unemployed, the unchurched, the unsaved.

Dad was truly a foot soldier in Christ's army and could pack a pew better than anyone. He helped launch mission churches in Huber Heights, Ohio, when he was based at Wright-Patterson Air Force Base, and in our hometown of Louisville, Kentucky.

"Jesus said, 'I will make you fishers of men,'" echoes from the square, wooden pulpit in my mind.

* *

Dad's glaring fault was that he was "too nice." He was a gentleman with an emphasis on gentle, exhibited by a story he once told me about his days in the Navy. A gunner on the USS *Caperton*, called one of the "fightingest destroyers in the Pacific Theater," he earned battle stars for his efforts in exotic-sounding places like Kwajalein, Truk, Saipan, Palau, Yap and Woleai. He came face to face with at least one Kamikaze pilot. As a kid, probably after watching the Pearl Harbor movie *Tora! Tora! Tora!*, I excitedly asked him if he'd killed anyone. "Did ya, Dad? Did ya?"

"You know, Steve, I'd like to think that I didn't," he said with a pause, "but I certainly *was* aiming at them."

While in the Navy, Dad had three front teeth knocked out in a one-sided fight with one of his shipmates.

"He punched out your teeth?" I asked. "What did you do to him?"

"Nothing," Dad said.

"Nothing?" I was amazed. "He punched out your teeth and you did nothing?"

"Well," Dad said. "He'd had too much to drink, and he clearly thought I was someone else."

"But," I asked. "Nothing?"

"It was an honest mistake," he said.

That was Dad. Nice—often too nice.

"That's your dad, all right," Mom said after hearing the story yet again. "He was always thinking of everyone else and never about himself."

Seriously, Dad never said anything disparaging about anyone—even those who blatantly took advantage of his good nature (it was really rather annoying)—and when others did, he would often try to defend those he heard being run down. "I understand you're mad, but have you thought that maybe he's having a bad day? Maybe he's not had all the advantages you've had."

Or as in a quote from Tim: "I'd guess this fella was having a real bad day, so he looked around for someone who was having a better one." Guess what? Tag, you're it.

In my rare visits to Dad's workplace, either at the US Army Corps of Engineers or an emerging company that built hospitals, his uncluttered desk was always stuck in some out-of-the-way, leftover spot. He never had a corner window office. He never had a window. No brass nameplate on the door. No secretary. Men half his age spoke condescendingly to him without the benefit of an angry retort. No snappy comeback.

I can remember once mistaking Dad's sweet disposition for cowardice. How could someone not only walk away from an unprovoked assault but simply discount the entire affair as an honest mistake? He held no grudge, sought no revenge.

He was a conundrum for sure, but a coward? Hardly. That issue, if there ever was any lingering doubt in my mind, was resolved one sunny Saturday afternoon in the late summer between the sixth and seventh grades. We—Mom, Dad and I—were getting ready for dinner when Benny, one of my class-mates who often had bad days and clearly had few, if any, of the advantages I had been afforded, scurried onto our back deck, screaming for Dad to come quick.

"He's gonna kill her!" Benny screamed. "I just know he's gonna kill her!"

Without a word, Dad was up from the dinner table, where he was glancing at the paper, and out the back door. He and Benny sprinted across the two backyards that separated Benny's house, a limestone ranch on the corner, from ours. Dad and Benny disappeared into the darkness of the garage as I trailed a backyard behind.

When I reached the screen door that separated the family's

pristine garage and the brightly lit kitchen, Benny's shirtless father, a muscled, darkly tanned Korean War veteran, was astride Benny's beehive-blonde mother on the kitchen floor. His bare knees pinned her thin shoulders against the white linoleum; her long, spindly legs were Barbie-Doll stiff. He held the barrel of his .45-caliber service pistol flush to her forehead.

Benny, a lanky, greasy-haired 12-year-old, stood to his father's right, shoulders slumped, visibly shaking.

Dad was to the left of Benny's mom. He was lying down on the floor. He spoke softly up to Benny's dad; so softly that I couldn't hear a single word of what he said. For what seemed like hours, but probably was more like 15 or 20 minutes—every second a lifetime—the four of them held the same positions, three of them silent, and I stood, motionless, just outside the oak-framed screen door.

As I remember the scene, it is reminiscent of a Civil War wax museum, maybe Robert E. Lee's surrender to Ulysses S. Grant at Appomattox Court House or Abraham Lincoln's private box at Ford's Theatre with John Wilkes Booth lurking in the shadows. All of the figures focused on a single point. None of them moving, but you can swear they're alive.

Dad continued to talk, softly.

Finally, Benny's father, whose back glistened with sweat, nodded. It was a slight nod, but it appeared to indicate that he acknowledged something Dad had said. Dad reached over slowly and took the semi-automatic pistol into his meaty hands. As I watched in amazement, Dad nonchalantly turned away from the trio and expertly removed the ammo clip as Benny's father disengaged his knees and rolled onto the floor away from Dad and next to his battered wife.

"Wait for me at home," Dad said calmly, acknowledging me for the first time outside the screen door. "Tell Mom I'll be along. Now go."

I went, half running across the two backyards and into our own. I have no memory of telling Mom what had happened up the street at Benny's house, and I have no recollection of her ever asking me. Dad returned home an hour or so later, alone.

"Everything all right?" Mom asked as he came in the back door.

"A misunderstanding," Dad said.

We ate skillet-fried chicken, green beans cooked with bacon, and Mom's butter-slathered mashed potatoes as if nothing significant had happened. After dinner we watched *Hee Haw* and sang along during the appropriate parts, as we always did.

> *Gloom, despair and agony on me-e!*
> *Deep dark depression, excessive misery-y!*
> *If it weren't for bad luck I'd have no luck at all!*
> *Gloom, despair and agony on me-e-e!*

> *Where oh where are you tonight?*
> *Why did you leave me here all alone?*
> *I searched the world over*
> *And thought I found true love*
> *You met another and*
> *Phhft you were gone.*

Then came *All in the Family, M*A*S*H, Mary Tyler Moore, Bob Newhart,* and *Carol Burnett*. As Saturday nights went, in all other regards, it was fairly typical.

Over the next few weeks, it became obvious that Benny and his mother were gone from the limestone house on the corner. When school started back in late August, Benny, one of our grade's better kickball players, was nowhere to be found.

Benny's father remained there for maybe six months after the kitchen showdown. When we'd pass him doing yard work in our aging Country Squire station wagon, he'd embarrassedly nod at Dad, but as far as I know they never spoke again, and Dad never spoke about it. Not a word. His proclamation to Mom, "a misunderstanding," is all I ever heard him say on the subject.

* *

In my 40 years as Dad's youngest son, I rarely heard him raise his voice, and he never once cussed. The closest he came was during one of our many Florida vacations when, north of Tarpon Springs, Dad had the amazing misfortune of reeling in an 18-inch-long monster of a fish that we learned later was called *Clarias batrachus*, or "walking catfish," a freshwater, air-breathing creature that is found mostly, almost exclusively, in Southeast Asia. It can best be described as a cross between a bloated water moccasin and an enlarged wedge of inner tube, black speckled with muted silver spots.

Dad unsuccessfully attempted to remove the hook from the fish's mouth before accidentally dropping it to the ground. Before he could pick it up, the beast lifted itself on its pectoral fins and started strutting, at first toward the water, then about-face and toward us, its head thrown back like an angry dog, which sent us both scurrying backwards onto the hood of Dad's then-new 1968 Country Squire wood-paneled station wagon. "That's the darndest thing I've ever seen," Dad said as the creature turned again and shimmied into the murky water, taking Dad's hook, line, and lure with it. Dad clipped the line and waved farewell from the hood of the car. For a moment, just an instant, I thought maybe Dad said damndest, but I'm fairly certain it was darndest, damn it.

For years when Dad and I told the story, we were greeted with rolled eyes and spiteful sighs of disbelieving disgust. If such a ghastly creature—a walking catfish—did exist, which most were certain it did not, how did it get from the Mekong Delta to an isolated swamp off US Highway 19?

It turns out that walking catfish were imported from Thailand by Florida fish farmers. In early 1968, it became illegal to possess them in captivity, and the fish farmers clandestinely released the fish into the bayous off the Gulf of Mexico. History should reflect that Dad, sporting plaid green, white, and yellow Bermuda shorts, matching shirt and a nice white mesh cap, was apparently one of the first amateur anglers to catch one, and I, wearing a smaller-sized duplicate ensemble, was the first witness.

While *Clarias batrachus* doesn't truly walk—upright, at least—it can shake and wiggle, a kind of strut, out of water for a mile or more as long as it remains moist. It normally lives in stagnant ponds and swamps, which often can be prone to drying up, which would leave a fish that did not possess the ability to migrate high and, most unfortunately for the fish, dry.

In my memory of the event, as Dad drove us back to Mamaw's house in New Port Richey, I stared out the window, dumbfounded by what we had seen. I can still hear Dad's voice: "Well, Stevie, my boy, that just goes to show, you never know what's going to happen."

More than four decades have passed since the encounter with *Clarias batrachus*. Father-and-son fishing trips between my son and me are rare. While I seldom, due in part to my lack of focus, caught much of anything with Dad, Christopher, to my knowledge, has never even gotten a bite with me.

* *

Dad died in 2002 en route home from Florida. He and Mom were returning from a semiannual pilgrimage to Clearwater, best known today as the headquarters of the Church of Scientology, to check in on Mamaw. Tim played the role of chauffeur. Dad and Tim were talking when somewhere just south of Cartersville, Georgia, Dad started slurring his words.

At the local hospital, the staff confirmed that Dad apparently had experienced a "small" stroke. He suffered a much more severe one while being transported by ambulance to the Redmond Regional Medical Center, a 230-bed acute care facility 29 miles west in Rome, Georgia, which, like its Italian namesake, is built on seven hills with a river running though it.

"He knew what was going on when they put him in the ambulance," Mom said. "I'll never forget it. He looked so scared. I don't think I'd ever seen him scared before."

When I think about it, the closest thing I saw to Dad being scared was the encounter with the walking catfish.

On the morning of Dad's strokes, he'd eaten in Valdosta at the Cracker Barrel—his favorite roadside eatery—and flirted with a young waitress he had first met on the trip to Florida 10 days before. They exchanged corny jokes and hugs, which were among Dad's favorite things. Dad could rattle off the personal histories and career aspirations of more than a dozen Cracker Barrel waitresses along Interstates 64, 65, 40 and 75. "Rose is working at Cracker Barrel in Franklin, Kentucky, to raise enough money to go back to cosmetology school down in Nashville," he would report. "She had to drop out when Neil, her baby's daddy, dropped out of sight."

My father loved these stories the way some women love soap operas. He cared about how the stories might resolve themselves. And he cherished the ladies, from the desk clerk at the Holiday Inn, where he swam laps for exercise, to the pharmacist who filled the half-dozen prescriptions typical of an 80-year-old man; but none more than my mother, a neighbor's granddaughter he married after only one formal date and a year's worth of letters between the South Pacific and northern Kentucky.

My first glimpse of my parents' lifelong passion came when I was 13 or 14 years old, which, by my math, meant they had been married more than 30 years.

I was sitting in the family room watching television, reruns of either *McHale's Navy* or *Gilligan's Island*, and over my right shoulder my mother had just started fixing dinner in the kitchen, which was separated from the family room by a countertop.

Dad, who could often be gregarious for a Southern Baptist deacon, was most often reserved. Apparently unaware of my presence, Dad strolled through the back door from work and ambled up behind my darkly exotic, curvaceous mother. He wrapped his arms around her. He spun her around, grabbed her hips, and began to hoist her onto the kitchen countertop.

He loudly nibbled on her neck and mumbled something, which I can only assume was rather frisky, into her ear. I thought I heard the words "tongue" and "hot" used together, but I'm not exactly sure. My mother's faux shock, "Oh, Harold," alerted him to my presence—some six to seven feet away.

Dad and I made eye contact over the countertop. My father blushed. He reluctantly released my mother from his grip and withdrew to another part of the house. Where Dad went, I'm not sure. He didn't come out of hiding for quite a while. We never spoke of it again.

*   *

When Dad was embarrassed, he would turn tomato-red, which was accentuated by his blond hair and fair features.

Sometime during the sixth grade, the physical education teacher showed a certain educational film in health class. A note was sent home to our parents to let them know that we would be seeing the film, and we might have questions when we got home. I can still remember Dad sheepishly coming into the backyard where I was playing whiffle-ball, having apparently been forced by Mom to have the ever-important "talk" with me.

"Well. Ugh. Well. I understand you saw a film at school today," Dad blundered, seizing an opportunity between innings.

"Yes," I said. "We did."

"Any questions?" Dad asked.

"I don't think so," I said.

"Good," he said as he returned to the safety of the house, never to mention the film or the topic again.

* *

When Tim called from Georgia to say that Dad was being taken to the hospital, northwest Georgia's "primary stroke center," I had just sat down for dinner. Around the crowded wooden table sat my wife, my 11-year-old son, and my three daughters—Katy, eight, Molly, five, and one-year-old Sydney. As Tim stammered the briefest of details of the severity of what was going on in Georgia, I responded in one- and two-word statements.

"Okay," I said.

"I understand," I said.

"I see," I said.

As I prepared to hang up the phone, Molly grabbed my hand.

"Dad," she said.

Aware that I was not paying attention to her, she said again, louder, "Dad."

Still, I was not focused.

"Steve," she said, catching me off guard by using my first name.

She pulled me close. She looked me square in the eyes and said, "Well, that just goes to show, you never know what's going to happen."

I was stunned. I visibly staggered. My mind was a swirl of incomplete tasks. Where is my cell phone? Would Mike, my other brother, still be at work? What had Molly said? Why did she call me Steve? Where should we exit to get to Rome, Georgia, the quickest? "Rome isn't near the interstate," I thought. How could Molly say something like that when I hadn't given the slightest indication of what was happening at the other end of the phone?

"Molly, what did you say?"

"I said 'It just goes to show that you never know what's going to happen.'"

Dad's words. She'd said, with no knowledge of the news I'd just heard, *exactly* what my Dad had said hundreds of times.

"Molly," I said. "You really shouldn't talk about things you don't know anything about. It's rude."

"Well," she said, smugly, confidently, arrogantly, "If I had said that the last time you *saw* Granddad was the last time you'd *see* Granddad, you wouldn't have believed me, now would you?"

I slumped in my chair, struggled to finish my dinner, and spent most of the next 90 minutes staring straight ahead, silent, stunned. Had I even said Dad's name? Had I given any indication anything was wrong? Life continued around the table and around me as normal. Alone in a funk, I stared at a chip in the freshly painted white pantry door.

During the more than six-hour drive to northwest Georgia with Mike and his wife, I tried to relax. I tried to engage them both in conversation and listen to songs on the radio, but I couldn't get the exchange with Molly out of my head. "Just goes to show . . ." weren't Molly words. Could Dad be trying, through Molly, to tell me something? Not possible, I said. "Now you're just being delusional," I told myself. "What are you Steve, daft?"

* *

Upon reaching the second-floor waiting room of the Redmond Regional Medical Center, we were greeted with my mother's muffled pronouncement that my nearly 81-year-old father was not going to make it. "I'm pretty sure he's already gone," she said. The second stroke Dad had suffered while in transport from Cartersville had filled his skull with blood, drowning his brain.

Dad was still alive, but only through the help of a ventilator. We were told that, once he was removed from the machine, his blood-oxygen levels would quickly drop and, within minutes, he would truly be gone.

Before being ushered into the brightly lit, starch-white intensive care unit, we were warned by his highly capable male nurse that he might not "look himself."

"You may not recognize him," someone, I think it was the nurse, said.

Other than the lights, the wires, and the chugging machines, Dad looked pretty much the way I remembered him always looking. He really hadn't aged much since the age of 40, when I was born. Yes, he had a little extra gray with the blond. He sat upright in the bed, his head tilted back and his mouth wide open.

"Harold, you're going to catch flies," Mom would say as he struck this same pose when watching Saturday night television in his easy chair back home in Kentucky. That chair, then maroon, was inherited from Aunt Laurie, a woman to whom we were not related. Re-upholstered later in a gold fabric, it's the chair in my bedroom in which I do most of my writing.

"Harold, you sleepin'?" Mom would ask.

"Nawp, Marge. Just resting my eyes."

So Dad looked pretty natural, all in all. Well, there was the white paper gown he was wearing, that was different. And the wires. And the little rubber tubing.

We were advised to take leave of him. We were told that they believed Dad could still hear us. He was feeling no pain but couldn't respond because his nerves had been drowned in blood.

Mom said this would be my chance to make peace with Dad. I could get whatever I wanted off my chest. It was my last chance to clear the air.

It was an opportunity I did not need. Didn't she know that? How could she think otherwise? Did we really need to dredge up the newspaper routes I signed up for that he had to deliver? Or Frisky, the tricolored husky mix I adopted in the weeks before leaving for college that he had to care for and feed? I thought not.

Did I really need to come clean about the Great Pellet Rifle Incident of 1978?

In the spring near the end of my sophomore year of high school, months after I'd gotten my coveted driver's license, I had taken the Country Squire a couple of blocks to Bruce's house for a birthday party. One of Bruce's gifts was a pellet rifle. At some point we—I, yes, I—became compelled with an over-whelming desire to test the "shatterproof" guarantee stamped on one of Dad's car windows. The first shot glanced off harm-lessly. "See," I said, "My dad works for the government, and they have special glass." The second shot, however, sent dozens of spider-web fissures through the entire passenger-side panel, leaving the window looking like a mosaic of greenish-blue stupidity.

When I slowly pulled the Country Squire into the driveway,

I hoped that Dad, who was working in the yard, wouldn't notice.

"Oh my goodness, what happened to the window?" he asked.

"Some idiot shot it out with a pellet rifle," I said.

"Where?"

"Uhhm, over near Bruce's house," I said without hesitation. "Yes, over near Bruce's house."

For the next 60 minutes, Dad and I drove back and forth through the neighborhood around Bruce's house looking for the idiot with the pellet rifle, but as thoroughly as Dad and I searched, we never found him.

Other than those adolescent infractions, for which I was certain any apology was long past the statute of limitations, I had nothing—absolutely nothing—to say.

Dad and I had spoken on the phone or in person no less frequently than every other day for the decade leading up to his death. We had long since traded our tattered fishing poles for vintage yard-sale golf clubs and played on a fairly regular basis. Granted, we fared little better golfing on the fairways than we did fishing in remote swamps and ponds or off of bridges or piers. Dad and I made fun of each other's lack of skills. We teased each other, but we continued to play the game originated in 15th-century Scotland with clubs nearly as old.

We told the same lame jokes over and over again. "Do you know why it's important to take two Baptists with you when you go fishing?" I would ask. "No, why?" he'd respond, again and again, no matter how many times he'd heard it. "'Cause if you take only one, he'll drink all your beer."

"Oh, that's a good one," he'd chuckle. "I need to remember that one."

"Jesus and Moses went golfing . . ."

"Oh, I love that one, especially when Moses parts the water to get Jesus's ball."

* *

In the history of man, or at least the Southern Baptist Church, there was no worse singer than Dad—well, at least, until I came along. This didn't stop either of us from trying. "The Bible says we should make a joyful noise unto the Lord," Dad would say. Well, that was what it was—noise. We could both butcher "Come to the Church in the Wildwood," the song Dad is crooning in my earliest childhood memory, beyond holy recognition.

Our inability to sing, at least on key, was one of the things we shared. Another was our trove of cornpone humor, at least until, in the months before that final trip to Florida, Dad lost the ability to deliver a punch line.

"There was a Baptist minister, a Catholic priest, and a Jewish rabbi," he'd begin. Then he'd pause. "Well, they did something. It had something to do with a goat, or was it, maybe, a banjo? Whichever, you'd have liked it."

I should have known then that Dad was slipping, because when it came to telling jokes, he was a maestro. "One day two hillbillies went fishing and were just reeling them in one after another. When it came time to quit for the day, the one hillbilly said to the other, 'It sure would be nice if we could mark our spot so we could come back here again sometime.' The second hillbilly said, 'I know, I know, we can paint a big X in the bottom of the boat.' The first hillbilly responded, 'You ain't too smart, are ya? Who's to say we'll get the same boat?'"

* *

Maybe if I had been more attentive to Dad's mental slippage, someone could have stepped in and helped. Maybe not. Beyond his newly acquired inability to deliver a punch line, there were other signs. In the week before the final journey to Florida, he'd complained of a headache and had been to see one of his many doctors. When we talked on the phone, he said, "I told him we were going on a little vacation, and he suggested I see the urologist when we get back."

Urologist? I guess, I thought, kidney stones *could* cause a headache. Dad battled kidney stones more than once and the thought of the pain they caused him and thinking about them now certainly gives me a headache.

Had Dad misheard the doctor? Had the doctor said neurologist? Did the doctor see signs of things to come?

My first indication he wasn't as sharp as he once was had come a year earlier on yet another trek to Florida. This time I was the chauffeur. Dad rented a large white van, and my entire family, including then-newborn Sydney, went to see Mamaw at the assisted living facility she had recently moved to in Clearwater, near her On Top of the World condo. We were on Interstate 75, headed south, between Athens and Chattanooga, Tennessee. Dad was riding shotgun.

"I wonder how much further it is to Chattanooga?" Dad asked.

"Well, Dad," I said, with a condescending tone in my voice, "we just passed exit 49, and that mile marker says 48, so I'd venture an educated guess that we're roughly 48 miles from Chattanooga."

"Huh, hum," he said as if pondering some newly acquired knowledge. "You mean the exit numbers correspond to the mile markers? So, the mile markers measure the distance from some fixed location?"

"Yes, Dad," I said. "I'd guess maybe the state line, just west of Chattanooga."

"That's really something," he said.

Yes, it was something—something Dad had taught me when I was little, along how to properly read a map, the correct thickness of interstate concrete and the per-mile construction costs. He also taught me how to score a baseball game and how to play chess, just not well enough that I could ever beat him.

* *

At the time of his death, Dad and I were beyond being a father and son; we were pals. He knew me, or at least he thought he did, and I knew him to the extent he was willing to share. As far as true issues, points of contention, there was nothing left unsaid. How could Mom not know that?

Maybe I should have thanked him more. Yes, I should have thanked him more. When my time alone with Dad came, the best I could muster was that he didn't need to worry; I knew all of his computer passwords, and I would take good care of his online fantasy baseball team for the rest of the season. His team, named the TamAmNets in tribute to his three oldest granddaughters—Tammie, Amanda and Lynette—had a good chance of making the playoffs. I also said I would e-mail all of his online friends and let them know that he was gone.

When the end finally came, as the doctors, nurses and nurse's aides had dutifully explained, almost exactly as they had explained it, the blood-oxygen numbers started to fall: eighties, seventies, sixties. Somewhere in the fifties, his body arched from the hospital bed and his grip on my hand became surprisingly, almost alarmingly, intense. Had we made a mistake letting them take him off the ventilator? Was he trying to hang on, or was he just, as I now believe, maintaining physical contact as long as possible? Forties. Thirties. His mouth, which had been hanging open, closed. I stuttered that I loved him, something I knew he knew without me telling him. Twenties. Teens. His grip still strong, his face began to compress and visibly shrank. There was a shudder I'll never forget, and he was gone.

*   *

After Dad died, I found a yellowed newspaper clipping in his tooled-leather wallet. It was a clipping of a section of a Ralph Waldo Emerson poem, unattributed.

> *Finish each day and be done with it.*
> *You have done all that you could.*
> *Some blunders and absurdities no doubt crept in;*
> *Forget them as soon as you can.*
> *Tomorrow is a new day:*
> *Begin it well and serenely and with too high a spirit*
> *to be encumbered with your old nonsense.*

Dad never dwelled on the past. "Finish each day and be done with it." That was the way he dealt with the day he disarmed Benny's father. "You have done all that you could."

If coaxed, Dad would talk about his childhood, his parents,

his wartime service, but only in the scantest of detail. He was far more interested in the here and now.

He didn't have a "bucket list" like in the movie—you know, those things you'd like to do before you "kick the bucket." From all accounts, he had seen all he wanted to see and had done all he wanted to do. "I know he'd have liked to have seen your kids graduate from high school," Mom said years later, "but, no, I don't think he left anything undone."

*   *

The drive home from Georgia to Louisville took seven silent hours with a dinner stop at—despite Mom's repeated requests for Cracker Barrel—Davy Crockett's Roadhouse in Nashville, Tennessee. By the time we reached Louisville, Dad, who had taken a Delta flight out of Atlanta, had made his way to the Nunnelley Funeral Home ahead of us. There were plans to be made, an obituary to write, and friends to alert.

The following afternoon, Brother Phelps, the recently called pastor at the Baptist church Mom and Dad had attended nearly every Sunday for roughly 30 years, visited the house to discuss plans for the funeral service. As it turned out, the church had, during its Wednesday night prayer services, been asking select members of the congregation to deliver a short testimonial on how they came to be a part of the church. On the Wednesday night before Mom and Dad left for Florida, Dad had gone to the midweek service alone. The man who was supposed to give his talk that night didn't show up and the pastor asked Dad if he minded filling in. "Well, of course not," Dad said.

He then gave a 15-minute, impromptu talk.

"Would it be okay if we used part of what Brother Harold said during the service?" Brother Phelps asked.

"Certainly," we all said.

Then we discussed which hymns would be sung. A group of young ladies had asked if they could sing "Amazing Grace."

"Certainly," Mom said. "Harold certainly loved 'Amazing Grace,' and Harold certainly loved young ladies."

Mom's biting wit can be abrupt and disarming all at the same time. It's a trait I've been told I inherited.

"Oh, Marge," Dad would have said if he'd been sitting there.

For the next 48 hours, well-wishers filed through the funeral home. "Why two days?" asked my wife. "Wouldn't one day be enough?" It wouldn't have been. There were people from a dozen different churches, the Baptist church association, the Gideons, members of a half-dozen different Sunday school classes he had taught over the years. There were members of Little League baseball teams and church softball and basket-ball teams Dad had coached and friends, even of mine, with whom he had associations and friendships, separate from any of which I was aware. The Holiday Inn desk clerk was there, bank tellers, his pharmacist. There were even friends from the Internet and, I kid you not, a pair of mournful Cracker Barrel waitresses. I half expected, somewhere in my subconscious, Benny might show up.

"Dad was so fortunate," I said over and over again, repeating what eventually became my funeral-home mantra. "You know, the morning he died, Dad went to Cracker Barrel, had his favorite breakfast and flirted with the waitresses. I just hope, I pray, that I can be doing the things I most enjoy the morning of the day that I die."

In the midst of the swirling mass of visitors, the weight of well wishing began to catch up with me and, for the first time in several days, I sat down.

I was joined on the ornate funeral parlor couch by a faceless, unidentified man who, seeing my grief, wanted urgently to tell me how lucky I was "to feel this bad."

"Lucky?" I said.

"Yes, lucky. Just think how many people lose a father and can't feel as bad as you feel. Take comfort in that. Some people feel nothing at all. Or worse, some people feel relief."

*   *

The morning of the funeral, August 1, was hot and muggy, which is typical for this time of year in the humid Ohio River Valley. The red-brick Southern Baptist church was packed with friends dad had made over the years. Many of the faces were the same as those from the previous two days of visitation, but others were new. In the vestibule, I was reunited with David, a member of Dad's first "junior boys" Sunday School class, and numerous members of his current class of "senior men:" Mr. Ray, Mr. Quiggins, Mr. Carter, Mr. Nall, Mr. Yates.

My eldest children, Christopher and Katy, then eleven and eight, had gone to Lutheran church camp in Indiana while I was away in Georgia. They came home early from camp for the funeral but missed the marathon visitation. Neither of them had, at that point in their lives, ever been in the presence of an open casket, a dead body. Neither of them was prepared to see Granddad, as they knew him, on public display.

What is it they say? "He looks so good; he looks so natural." Dad did. He looked much more "natural" in front of the church than he did those some-odd days before in Georgia, in the white paper gown, with the life drawn out of him.

The first speaker was Mark, the associate pastor, a young seminary student within months of being an ordained minister. He presented a summation of Dad's biography. It was nice.

The young ladies, as scheduled, sang "Amazing Grace." It was lovely.

Pastor Phelps then delivered a sermon based on the 11th chapter of Acts, the 24th verse: *for he was a good man, full of the Holy Spirit and of faith.*

"I think you would expect me to say he was a good man, but Harold Vest *was* a good man: a good husband, a good father, a good grandfather, a good friend, and a good neighbor. He was a good man."

Then there was a long, heart-felt prayer and more music.

No one, however, was prepared for the speaker who came next.

When the pastor had asked if they could use some of what "Brother Harold" said during his Wednesday night testimonial the week before the trip to Florida, we all naturally assumed they were going to pull some quotes from what he said.

As we sat uncomfortably in the hard-backed pews, Dad lay in profile under the pulpit from which he had, for three decades, delivered the Sunday morning announcements. Grief fell upon me like a cloud.

In the week before the final Florida trip, Dad had specifically asked if we could bring Christopher over so he could take him out for the day, swim laps at the Holiday Inn pool and treat him to dinner. "It's important to me," Dad said. What they discussed is between them. All Christopher has ever shared with me is that he—my dad—and he—my son—were very much alike beyond their blond hair and thin, strong frames. "He said that I reminded him of himself when he was my age," Christopher said.

I've often asked Christopher for more details but have never gotten very far.

What advice Dad may have given Christopher is beyond my reach, but I can remember Dad giving me unsolicited advice only a pair of times. Once was when I was 14 and particularly smitten with a petite brunette, a member of the youth group in the same church where we again found ourselves. He said, "She's a pretty young lady, but before you get too serious with any girl, you want to take a good, long look at her mother. That's all I can say—take a good, long look at her mother."

Whether Dad's sage words were based on his observation of the girl-in-question's mother or personal experience related to Dad's long-suffering dealings with his mother-in-law, my grandmother, Mamaw, can never be clarified. "What in the world possessed you two to have three children is beyond me," I can hear Mamaw saying right now. "Harold, are you daft?"

The other slice of advice: "Don't eat your ice cream too fast—it'll give you a headache."

The sweltering August sun shining through the clear panes of the stained-glass windows glimmered off Dad's steel-blue casket. My other important questions would never be answered. Where had Dad gotten his fortitude? What was his secret?

Mixed with my grief were growing pangs of jealousy. Dad had shared more details with strangers along the interstate than he had with me. He had imparted some secret message to my son, who, now that I think of it, is the one called upon—not me—when the kind of impromptu prayer Dad used to give is needed before meals when the extended family is gathered. When my friends meet my son, a stunned look comes over their faces. How can a father and son be this different? It's the same look Dad's friends had after talking with me. If Dad and Christopher are, were, as much alike as Dad claimed, does that make me the conundrum?

If I were to answer this question, I needed more information, but for me it was too late to get Dad's story.

For all of my efforts, what I had, I knew, was a collection of short, pithy parts of a greater whole that I still could not see. Dad had taught me during our brief interest in model ships and airplanes that the builder first must determine if he has all the needed parts before starting on a project. "I'm not sure you have the patience required," he said.

You don't want to spend hours or days on a model or a puzzle only to find that something vital is missing. As much effort goes into an incomplete job as does a complete one, only without the satisfaction. "No one else may know that it's just not right, but you will, promise."

That's the beauty of writing: You can leave parts out, even important ones, and it can at times add, not detract, from the story. Important pieces—yes. Crucial ones—doubtful. Writing isn't math. It can add up or not—either way is fine as long as it is, like an omelet, done well.

"I was born on the banks of the Dismal Swamp," echoed through my scrambled consciousness via the church sound system. I fiddled with a visitor's information card which, if I had filled it out, might have prompted a long-distance visit by

Dad's successors on the visitation committee. "Oh, that's all I need," I thought, sarcastically.

None of us—not me, not Mom, not Mike, not Tim—knew that Dad's testimonial, delivered impromptu the Wednesday night before they—Mom, Dad and Tim—left for sunny Florida, had been recorded for posterity.

"Oh, they're not really," I muttered, hearing a slight crackle over the sound system, but not finishing my own statement. Oh, yes they were.

The high-definition quality sound of Dad's voice, coupled with the sight of his lifeless body only a few yards away, left me doubled over as if I'd been sucker punched by a drunken sailor staggering back from a booze-filled shore leave on the island of Saipan.

"I was born on the banks of the Dismal Swamp," began a testimonial that covered much of my father's young life. Dad told stories that Wednesday night that I'd never heard before and didn't really hear at the time of the afternoon funeral. The shock of hearing Dad's voice left me partially deaf, the result of an emotional overdose that would not subside for weeks, maybe months, after the episode.

On the way out of the church, Tom, a college fraternity brother and a Catholic, stopped me and said, "Steve, I've never been to a Baptist funeral before. Does the deceased always speak?"

"Not . . . well, not that I've ever heard of," I stammered. "Tom, I don't think so."

Even though I didn't listen, I had heard enough to know that I now had the missing piece. Dad had delivered—certainly not in the manner I asked nor expected, but again, he had come through.

"That was interesting," said Sheryl, my wife's sister. "I've never been to a funeral where . . ."

"Neither have I, Sheryl," I said, "You know, I guess that just goes to show, you never know what's going to happen."

Six-year-old Molly played in the church nursery during the funeral. She never saw Granddad's body, and she missed his broadcasted speech, but she did go with us to the cemetery for the graveside service. As the two family limousines left the church, we were followed by two dozen cars in a procession that meandered from the South End of Louisville to Erlanger, Kentucky, in suburban Cincinnati, a distance of more than 95 miles. Mike, then a vehicle enforcement officer with the Commonwealth of Kentucky, had arranged for a highly out-of-the-ordinary police escort from the church to the graveside.

In which car Molly rode, I'm not sure.

When we arrived at the cemetery, Jason, the grandson of Dad's baby brother, Charles, Dad's lone living sibling, played "Amazing Grace" on his Appalachian dulcimer. Uncle Charles and his daughter were there. The US Navy sent three sailors in uniform, one of whom played "Taps." They fired rifles and presented Mom with the folded United States flag from Dad's casket. Friends and relations from Indiana, Ohio, and Kentucky were gathered in the sweltering hundred-degree heat. There were people there on the grassy cemetery hillside that neither of my parents nor I had seen in decades.

I stood in the grass directly behind Mom, who was seated in a padded folding chair. Molly stood to my right. As the sailors finished "Taps," Mom said, not speaking to anyone in particular, that she wished Dad had been able to see all the fuss everyone had made.

"He simply wouldn't have believed it. You know, Harold would have loved this."

Molly leaned forward, gently tapped Mom on her right shoulder.

"Marge," she said, calling my mother something other than Granny for the only time, before or since. With Mom's complete attention, much the way she had garnered mine the week before in our tiny kitchen, Molly's big brown eyes locked on Mom's, and she said in a hauntingly baritone voice, "It's okay, you know, Marge," pointing up, "there really are some mighty nice things up there, too."

CHAPTER 3

The Talk

THAT DAD CHOSE TO RETREAT into the house rather than give me the facts-of-life talk came as a relief, but not as a surprise.

Dad knew, I suspected, that I knew all I needed to know about the opposite sex.

The knowledge came from the extensive collection of *Playboys* my brother, Tim, had left behind while he was driving tanks and drinking beer in Germany. Dad never once saw me with one of Tim's magazines, boldly billed as "Entertainment for Men." They were hidden, neatly stacked, in chronological order in the bottom drawer of his small, black, three-drawer dresser that now resides in my daughter Katy's room.

Only when my parents were away and not scheduled to return for some time would I dare enter the sanctum of Tim's vacant lair and sneak a peek at the large, slick, saddle-stitched magazines.

As my parents' Country Squire station wagon backed out of the driveway, I watched until they disappeared around the curve and then I sprinted down the hall to (the room that was called) "the company room," although, other than Mamaw, I cannot recall anyone else ever staying in it. Tim's possessions were off limits, and any disruption would certainly ignite his wrath, which could be dangerously volatile and inappropriately explosive.

As compulsive as I was about making a beeline for that drawer, which I was sure held the mysteries of life, because of the way the images made me feel—my heart would race, my face would flush hot, and my mouth would get dry—I was equally obsessive in making sure these priceless, one-dollar magazines were always just as Tim had left them. Any disturbance in the order or manner of placement would leave me exposed as a young voyeur in need of a long, uncomfortable talking-to, possibly by someone more qualified, possibly licensed, to conduct such discussions.

I removed the heavy wooden drawer from the dresser so that I could easily access each magazine without scuffing it against the bottom of the upper drawer. I once overhead Aunt Mabel explaining how a seasoned cat burglar always begins with the lowest drawers in a dresser and works upward, allowing them to work more stealthily without opening and closing of drawers. I can't remember how she acquired such knowledge, but she was a worldly woman after all, a past Worthy Grand Matron of the Order of the Eastern Star.

With the desired drawer sitting on the gold-colored carpet, I would sit, poised on my knees with my feet under my hips, ready for this mysterious communion that gave me a strangely familiar feeling. The pictures were different, but the emotional response they brought out of me was similar to how I felt when looking through Sears' *Wish Book* for the things that Santa might bring.

While I was meticulous in covering up my emerging *Playboy* obsession, someone else was not. More than once I found a page folded incorrectly or a magazine out of its proper chronological sequence. Since I lived alone with Mom and Dad, I assumed it was Dad checking out the younger generation. I guess it could have been Mom, but I never asked, as it would have revealed my own guilt, my own covetous sin.

* *

I remember an event that occurred decades later, while I was working as an up-and-coming sportswriter—running into a respected basketball coach I knew in a less-than-high-class New Orleans strip club called the Bourbon Burlesque. It was during the NCAA Final Four, which is an anticipated sporting event for the rest of us, but a convention for those in the coaching fraternity. The young coach was mortified because he knew, at least momentarily, that his gig was up. His eyes flew open. The blood drained from his face. In that instant, he believed I was in the Bourbon Burlesque on a journalistic quest to expose his other life, a secret that would damage his well-tended reputation as a straight-shooting, churchgoing family man. That was in the instant before he realized I, too, was just there to see boobs.

* *

While Dad may have figured out my covert *Playboy* obsession, it was, like many things, never discussed. He never definitively confirmed what I believed that he suspected— that I had, as young as nine years old, learned much of what I needed to know from, among others, Danielle de Vabre, Miss November 1971.

From Danielle I learned that my kind of woman was roughly five-foot-five and weighed in the neighborhood of 120 pounds. Her measurements were 36-25-34, and such a woman could be found in Montreal, Canada.

Like me, doe-eyed Danielle aspired to be a writer. She wanted to put on paper the tale of "a young French-Canadian girl who spends a perfect winter as a ski instructor." On the other hand, I would, I was sure, write of the complexities of being snuggled by Danielle's ampleness in the quilted sleeping bag she peeks out of on the magazine's cover. The thought of the two of us kissing on the bearskin rug shown in her pictorial made me noticeably warm.

I knew Danielle's "turn-ons" were sports cars and skiing. More importantly, I learned that her "turn-offs" were dishonesty and conceit—two things I needed to avoid if I were to be successful in pursuit of her much-sought-after charms. I would also need to learn to ski (which I never did) and acquire a sports car (which I never have).

From Elaine Morton, Miss June 1970, I gleaned that I might not need to learn to ski or travel to Canada (she lived in Wichita Falls, Kansas), but I should never "chew food or talk" with my mouth open. I got the part about the food, but I never have been able to figure out how to successfully converse without opening my mouth.

From Carol Imhof, Miss December 1970, who lived in Chicago, which was even closer than Kansas, I learned to avoid "obsessive domination" and to seek cozy, rustic places. The thought of cozy, rustic places would draw me back to Danielle in that quilted sleeping bag, which would quickly prompt a return visit, deeper into the stack of Tim's magazines.

* *

What sort of man reads *Playboy*? "A young man riding the crest of the good life. A traveler whose sense of adventure knows no boundaries. Fact: *Playboy* is read by one of every two men under 35 (more than any other magazine)."

* *

In February 1973, when I was 11, around the time "The Film" was shown at school, I found my ideal two-dimensional woman. She was—as were Danielle, Carol and Elaine—five-foot-five. The three previous pretenders to the coveted crown of my affections had been various shades of brunette, while Cyndi, who matched my weight at 103 pounds, was blonde. Cyndi's measurements were 34-22-34. Her turn-on—she had only one—was "creative men."

In a confusing world where being tall, dark, and handsome pays rich, romantic dividends, I could be sure only of the dark part. I *do* tan easily. Creative—maybe I could muster that. Maybe finding love wouldn't require learning to ski or driving a sports car.

Cyndi's turnoff was irresponsibility. While I didn't know exactly what that was at the time, it was something I was certain I could avoid.

Her strength was that she was "honest and sincere and loyal. I'm also completely trusting and look for the good in everyone I meet."

Who wouldn't dream of holding Cyndi Wood's soft hands and kissing Cyndi Wood's smiling mouth? When she was selected as Playmate of the Year 1974, it confirmed, once and for all, at least in my young mind, that I had pretty good taste.

For those three years that Tim was away, I educated myself at every opportunity. I studied women's likes and dislikes, the way I should dress, and the type of stereophonic equipment I should have in my future high-rise bachelor pad.

It was clear that I would need to smoke any of a dozen brands of advertised cigarettes and drink copious amounts of alcohol, which was problematic for a Baptist. Drink or not, it was clear that my bar needed to be stocked with Smirnoff vodka, Dry-Dark Bacardi rum, Ballantine's scotch, either Seagram's Canadian Whiskey or Canadian Mist, Paul Masson brandy, Seagram's Extra-Dry gin, and Jim Beam and Old Grand-Dad bourbons.

To smell my manly best, I could use Brut like Dad, but I could also splash on colognes by Pub, Canoe and Chantilly, which promised to "shake her world."

Did *Playboy* inspire Dad's purchase of his first pair of Hush Puppies? Did it influence his decision to buy a Honeywell Pentax Spotmatic camera?

For me, I was going to need either some "funky" shoes from Dexter or some Roblee suit boots, Burlington socks, Jantzen shirts and striped slacks from either Lee or Jaymar. I would definitely need a 14k solid-gold Bulova watch.

Based on the ads, the best stereo receivers were by Pioneer or Panasonic, but if I wanted to get my lovely lady naked, I would need Sony CF-620, "handsomely housed in walnut-grained cabinetry."

In *Playboy*, I was introduced to the fiction of Kurt Vonnegut (one of Tim's favorite writers), Norman Mailer, and Jack Kerouac. While I couldn't appreciate it at the time—*Runaway Ralph* was more my speed—it was my first exposure to more serious literature.

It was there that I first heard of Shel Silverstein and LeRoy Neiman.

I studied the cartoon art of Alberto Vargas, Erich Sokol, Gahan Wilson and Eldon Dedini. I was most drawn to the women created by Doug Sneyd with their big eyes and sweet smiles. Sneyd's cartoons were the funniest, too, especially after I was old enough to understand them, such as one with a luscious summer theater waitress talking with an equally attractive actress outside Ye Boar's Head Tavern. "You did Shakespeare in the Park? Big deal—last week I did him in the hayloft."

I reveled in the big-breasted misadventures of *Little Annie Fanny*, and I memorized the jokes printed on the page following the Playmate of the Month section.

A doctor had sex with one of his patients and felt guilty the next day. No matter how hard he tried to forget about it, his shame and sense of betrayal were overwhelming. A reassuring voice in his head said, "Don't worry about it. You aren't the first medical practitioner to have sex with one of his patients."

But then he would hear another voice, one that jolted him back to reality. "You are a sick bastard," it whispered, "and a terrible veterinarian."

Whether Dad read the jokes, too, I don't know.

My college friends who attended law school learned that they should never ask a question to which they did not already know the answer. One thing I learned from Dad was to never ask a question to which the answer might be something you did not want to hear.

Careful not to blow my cover, in front of Dad I never told any of the scads of *Playboy* jokes I had memorized.

Have you heard the one about the night Mick Jagger, the lead singer of the Rolling Stones, spent in Chicago's Playboy Mansion? It was the middle of the night, and Mick was awakened by screams for help coming from the next bedroom. Mick leapt to his feet and rushed over and kicked in the door to find Hefner attempting to engage in an unwanted homosexual act with the Stetson-wearing actor Dennis Weaver. Mick, shocked and somewhat groggy, stuttered in protest, "Hey, Hugh . . . get off of McCloud."

I never heard Dad relay any of the jokes in my arsenal.

I did, however, notice a little extra attention on Dad's part whenever Barbi Benton appeared, as she did for five years, on *Hee Haw*, a staple in my parents' Saturday night television watching schedule.

Of all the women I studied, I knew five-foot-three, green-eyed Barbi most thoroughly. She was publisher Hugh Hefner's longtime girlfriend. I had analyzed Barbi's auburn-brown hair, her wickedly long eye lashes and her perfect teeth. I had moved my thin fingers over the images of her taut 34-23-34 figure and down her bronze, well-toned legs to her finely shaped feet, accented as they were in her Fred Slatten-designed six-inch heels. Yes, my beloved Cyndi Wood appeared in the film version of *M*A*S*H*, but it seemed for a while that Barbi Benton, beyond being just a *Hee Haw* Honey, was virtually everywhere. She was a regular on *Love Boat* and *Fantasy*

Island. She appeared on *Marcus Welby, M.D, Charlie's Angels, Murder, She Wrote* and yes, *McCloud*.

Barbi had her own half-hour television show, *Sugar Land*, for a while. *Sugar Land* lasted only 13 episodes, and somehow I never saw a single one. To have two of the sweetest substances, sugar and honey, both linked to Barbi is appropriate. In Hinduism, honey (*madhu*) is one of the five elixirs of immortality, and she had, without question, a timeless beauty. In Hindu temples, honey is poured over the deities in one sacred ceremony. Of all the Hee Haw Honeys, which included Misty Rowe, Gunilla Hutton, and Victoria Hallman, also known as Miss Honeydew, Barbi was the one I was most interested in pouring honey over and, heck, I'm not even Hindu.

"Has she been in something else?" I can hear Dad repeatedly asking the silent audience, which seldom included anyone other than Mom and me. "She sure does look mighty familiar."

CHAPTER 4

Mamaw Departs

OUR AUDREY HIT FLORIDA IN the spring of 1968. She blew out of northern Kentucky, just across the mighty Ohio River from Cincinnati, Ohio, leaving no bridge standing. Her departure came less than a year after the death of Mac, my grandfather, her husband.

There certainly was no going-away party, or at least none to which Mamaw was invited. If there was a celebration, it would have been at Mamaw's expense. Everyone she knew was daft, a fool, or a damned fool, and she refused to suffer any of them any longer. She sold her red brick, two-story house and most of her furniture. She bought a brand-new white-on-white 1969 Buick Skylark and a white ranch-style house in New Port Richey, Florida. I was almost seven.

* *

One of the people she was leaving behind was her next-door neighbor with whom she'd had an ongoing feud for years over everything from the varieties of flowers he grew in his yard to the clothes his children wore to the insults, real and imagined, they had each hurled in Mamaw's direction. "Oh, the things they say to me, you just wouldn't believe it." Then, without pause, "Why on earth would anyone with half a brain have four children? What in the world was he thinking?"

Mamaw had one child, Margie Doris, my mother. Everyone, after seeing the great example Mamaw set by stopping after one, should have followed suit. Anything else, she said, was "utterly ridiculous," "utterly utterly ridiculous," or "the most ridiculous thing I've ever seen. What are they, daft?"

When Mom's turn at motherhood came along, she said she would not, could not, inflict being an only child on her own children. She said the spotlight was too brutally intense. Being an only child made Mom feel isolated and desperately alone, especially when her father was away on the railroad and it was just her and Mamaw.

I could relate, being a dozen years younger than my closest sibling. I often felt alone even with my parents *and* Mamaw. "What on earth were they thinking?"

* *

From my earliest recollections, my parents' mode of operations on any given Saturday or Sunday afternoon was to pile into the car—whether it was the 1962 Ford Fairlane, the 1968 Country Squire station wagon or Mamaw's Buick Skylark—and go visiting.

"Let's go see Aunt Laurie," Mamaw might say, referring to her only lifelong friend. Aunt Laurie, a widow, lived alone atop a hill overlooking the Kentucky River, south of the state capital, less than a mile from the house I now call home. I remember several of our visits there, including one where Aunt Laurie deftly disarmed me when I picked up her loaded derringer pistol from a small round table in her living room, thinking it a toy.

I didn't learn until years later that the derringer, the favored tool of 19th century assassins such as John Wilkes Booth, was loaded, and Aunt Laurie wasn't an aunt at all. She was, instead, the type of sister Mamaw would have chosen if a family could have been drafted like a major league baseball team or recruited like a garden club—those who knew to hold their tongue no matter what was spewing from Mamaw's venomous mouth. They also had to be well dressed, clean, and preferably pale.

"We haven't seen Charles or Bill or Gladys in a while," Dad might suggest if he were brave, but it was, he knew, a remote alternative plan that would come into play only if all other efforts failed, and most times, not even then.

"Uhmph," Mamaw would snort at Dad's inappropriate proposal to visit *his* siblings, a waste of *her* valuable and limited time. "Uhmph."

Those visits, equally memorable for entirely different reasons, would need to wait until another Saturday or Sunday when Mamaw wasn't along.

"Well, Mother, shouldn't we check in on Aunt Lois or Aunt Lucille?" Mom would offer, since Aunt Lois was not only Mamaw's first cousin on her mother's side, but also her sister-in-law since she and Lois had married brothers. Aunt Lucille, who earnestly believed a large family lived in the rusted-out, discarded Chevy that adorned her front yard, was Mamaw's late husband's baby sister. Aunt Lucille lived alone—well, other than the people in the car—atop another scruffy rural hillside, 65 miles north.

"Uhmph. That's utterly ridiculous. Why in the world would we want to do that? Visit *them*? Good Lord, Margie, have you lost your mind, too?"

These trips with Mamaw, in my memory, occurred after

my brothers, 15 and 11 years my senior, had left home—Mike for the United States Marines and marriage, Tim for college and cold beer. "Can I please just stay home?" I'd plead as we were loading the car with heaven knows what. If I knew what was good for me, especially during Mamaw's three-week-long visits from Florida, I would be wise to keep my smart young mouth shut. "Pleeeease," I begged.

"Good lord, Margie, we can't take the boy with us and we can't leave the boy here. If you had stopped after Mike, like you should have, we wouldn't have to worry with this," Mamaw would argue. "There's no telling what kind of trouble he'll get into and then, oh good Lord, what will people say?"

I had not yet learned to keep my mouth shut. I still struggle with that skill today. Dad, however, was wiser, more experienced. In the roughly 35 years I witnessed, Dad uttered only a few dozen words, maybe a sentence or two, in Mamaw's presence.

"Margie, you're not going to let him wear that, are you?" she said, looking at me.

Following a brief, one-sided discussion and several failed attempts at dressing more appropriately, we would start out, generally—well, without exception—in the direction of Mamaw's choosing. We all knew Mamaw's way was the only way, and it was good to remember that. "Why would anyone in their right mind want to go there? To see *them*?" Mamaw would offer. "Uhmph."

It's important to understand that there were no advance letters, postcards or phone calls to warn anyone we might be dropping by. "We certainly don't want them sitting around waiting on us," Mamaw would reason. "That would simply be rude."

A visit from Mamaw was a precious gift. Anyone alerted of her pending arrival most certainly would go to an inappropriate amount of trouble and throw themselves into an unseemly fit. It was a courtesy, Mamaw reasoned, that she should arrive unannounced.

We would sometimes travel for hours and hundreds of miles over bumpy, twisted country roads only to find whomever not at home. "Well," she would say from the other side of the back seat she shared with my mother—on the good days—or (on the days I'd rather forget) me. "Oh, well. Harold, I guess you should leave them a note and let them know that we were here. Be sure to tell them we'll try again another time. I know they'll be oh-so disappointed to have missed us. Uhmph."

If Mamaw were particularly upset by her unexpected knock going unanswered, she might follow up her "uhmph" with an "oh, hell" or "damn," to which Mom would respond, "*Mother*," to which Mamaw would add another "uhmph."

We'd then putter away in search of our next unsuspecting beneficiary or drive back home, a trip that sometimes would again take hours and cover hundreds of miles. If we turned for home, I was, more often than not, relieved. I wanted to be at home, locked safely away in my bedroom.

My parents, having again not lived up to Mamaw's expectations, would be silently deflated. Mamaw, grandly indignant, was always vocally dejected.

How could anyone be so inconsiderate as to not be home to greet her? It was beyond Mamaw's comprehension, especially after all the effort she'd put into coming to see them. "We came all this way. The least they could do was be home," she'd say. "Well, then. See if they get a Christmas card from me this year. Uhmph."

In my memory, entire summers were spent this way.

* *

"Let's go see Mabel," Mamaw announced during breakfast one morning in Florida. I'm guessing I might have been nine at the time, no older than eleven. Of my great aunts, Mabel was my favorite. Mabel was her large family's rebel. As a widow in the late 1960s, she drove a brand-new turquoise Oldsmobile Delta 88. She had left home at 15 and married the chief of a crew that was constructing a road in front of her parents' home near Verona, Kentucky. She used that road to leave and never looked back. She and her husband Gus eventually landed in Florida. After his death, she built a small empire in the north-central Florida swamps. She lived in Gus's former hunting cabin, a small concrete-block house with an actual bearskin rug (snarling head and all) on the sandy banks of the Ocklawaha River. Near a hamlet named Eureka, Aunt Mabel lived with her big yellow dog, Sheba.

In contrast, Mamaw lived in an expansive development in Clearwater called On Top of the World, a collection of two- and three-bedroom condominiums. More than six thousand retirees over the age of 55 lived beyond the Arc de Triomphe, the gateway to World Parkway and its curbed side streets with names such as Franciscan, Brazilia and Rhodesian. Each building, while basically the same inside, bore the façade of an exotic, distant country: China, India, Denmark. Mamaw lived in the Old Spanish Building, a white building adorned with a faux mission-style terra cotta tile roof.

That morning, after a breakfast of tasteless cereal and lukewarm skim milk, we passed around *The Clearwater Times* and *The Tampa Tribune* while the four of us took turns getting in the shower.

"Reds won again," Dad announced.

"Uhmph," Mamaw answered.

We loaded into the Country Squire station wagon and began what then was then a three-hour-plus trek up US Highway 19, through Dunedin, Palm Harbor, Cove Springs, Tarpon Springs, New Port Richey, Hudson, and Hernando Beach, and then across country to the western edge of the Ocala National Forest, established two years after Mamaw was born, making it the oldest such forest east of the Mississippi River.

"Why in the world Mabel lives all the way out here, I'll never know," Mamaw snapped. "Good lord, whose bright idea was this anyway?"

"Yours, mother," Mom said.

"Uhmph," Mamaw grunted. "Harold, are you sure you're going the right way?"

"Yes, Mamaw."

"Uhmph."

After passing through Weeki Wachee with its "World Famous Mermaids," Homosassa, Ocala, Silver Springs, and Fort McCoy, we arrived, unannounced, in Aunt Mabel's freshly graveled driveway sometime after noon.

Aunt Mabel, the second of Mamaw's three younger sisters, was a ceramics artist with her own industrial-sized kiln. She taught ceramics classes to a growing influx of housewives, snowbirds, and retirees from a cinderblock building Gus had built her on their extensive wooded property.

We arrived to find a dozen cars parked around the building, which was filled with two dozen ladies from the surrounding community, all working on various projects, mostly ceramic ashtrays and statuary depictions of pink flamingos, green frogs, and alligators.

As we unloaded the must-have items that accompanied us on each escapade, Sheba came down the driveway to greet me. She licked my ears and wagged her large frayed tail. Sheba was my compatriot. Then, dogs, like children, were to be seen and certainly not heard. That doesn't mean we didn't see and didn't hear. I'm sure Sheba had seen more than her share of human foolishness, to which she could express no opinion. We were silent and largely invisible witnesses.

I sat in the gravel petting Sheba. Aunt Mabel saw us through the cedar-trimmed screen door and excused herself momentarily from her students. As she came out of the building, Mamaw was coming up the driveway behind me. "YOO-WHOO, IT'S ME!" Mamaw yelled in a gleeful voice she employed upon her unexpected arrival, the only acknowledgement that someone *might* be surprised to see her. "IT'S ME, your sister Audrey, all the way from Clearwater."

Mom and Dad were still unloading the car. Baking soda, laundry soap, peanut butter, Ritz and graham crackers, bleach, baked beans, crossword puzzles, and seek-and-finds. Zest. Beach towels. Fishing poles. Matchbox cars and Hot Wheels. Melted crayons and coloring books. Oreo cookies. Pillows and blankets. Salt-water taffy. Cereal. Pancake mix. And an unwanted Stuckey Pecan Log for Mabel.

"It's great to see you," said Aunt Mabel, who I imagine knew all too well that greeting Mamaw required as much care as removing the fragile creations from her industrial-sized kiln.

"It's great to see you," Aunt Mabel's voice echoes to me across the decades.

I'm positive that's exactly what Aunt Mabel said. She couldn't have been more than 10 to 12 feet away from me when she said it. Aunt Mabel's pure white hair rose in a beehive, and her white-and-gold pantsuit had a timeless style that matched her demeanor. Other than being a few inches taller and two dozen pounds thinner, she was a mirror image of Mamaw, only a decade younger, minus the anger and hate.

Aunt Mabel paused for a thoughtful second and said something to the effect that her ceramics class had just started, but it would be over in roughly 30 minutes. "Once the class is over, we can all go for a nice lunch in Ocala or Silver Springs."

"Uhmpf," Mamaw said, exasperated that her baby sister would not just drop everything she was doing upon her arrival. Classes are canceled for hurricanes, aren't they?

Mamaw huffed something about not knowing she needed "a damned appointment." I couldn't quite hear that part with Sheba licking my ears.

But I did hear, "Well then! Uhmpf. If you don't have time for your own sister, you can just forget it."

Mamaw spun on the heels of her flat white shoes, one-hundred-eighty degrees, stomped down the driveway and returned to the back seat of the Country Squire. Speechless, my parents loaded the beans, bleach, baking soda and everything else back into the station wagon, and four of us, silent, returned to Clearwater, passing back through Ocala,

Hernando, Homosassa Springs, and a half dozen other towns. As far as I know, Mamaw and Aunt Mabel, living less than 150 miles apart, never spoke again.

"Uhmph . . . I have never been more offended in my entire life," Mamaw said, breaking the silence on the ride back to On Top of the World. "None of them, not a single damn one, ever appreciated all I did for them."

"Them:" her three brothers and three sisters, whom she believed should have treated her with more respect since she was forced to accept the responsibility of raising them by her "near worthless" mother.

From that day forward, we were forbidden to visit Aunt Mabel, who lived in or near Ocala, the "lightning capital of the world," until she died at 85 in 2001. On that clear day on the new driveway, some three decades earlier, Aunt Mabel was crossed off Mamaw's Christmas card list, which was like being purged from an exclusive collegiate sorority, never to be spoken of again.

* *

"Mamaw was just so jealous of Mabel," Mom told me years later. "She despised Mabel for living a better life. Your Aunt Mabel traveled the world. She once lived in Costa Rica. She was the Worthy Grand Matron of the Order of the Eastern Star."

From the teary-eyed manner in which Mom describes her mother, it's clear that I'm not the only one who struggled to understand Mamaw living in exile, completely isolated from those she considered her less-than-intelligent but nonetheless dutiful subjects. Mom attempts to explain Mamaw through parables such as one about shopping with Aunts Mabel and Naomi. "Mamaw was looking at a white blouse, but there weren't any in her size. Aunt Mabel, being thinner, then came along and was looking at the same blouse and it was in her size, but Mamaw spoke up and said, 'Oh, I was looking at that. You can't have it.' Mamaw bought it. She took it home, knowing it wouldn't fit, but she'd be damned if she was going to let Mabel have it."

The next day, after Mabel and Naomi had left, Mamaw returned the blouse, shocked that it didn't fit.

When I relayed my crystal-clear memory of the showdown in the driveway to Mom years later, she claimed that it never happened. "Well," she said, it had happened, but I certainly wasn't there to see it. Mamaw did go to see Mabel, but it was to pick up a set of white ceramic reindeer pulling Santa in his sleigh. Aunt Mabel had made a set for each of her sisters—Audrey, Alice and Naomi—and when Mabel called Mamaw and described it, Mamaw said she 'didn't want the damned thing.'"

"When Mother changed her mind a few weeks later, she and a neighbor drove to Mabel's to get it. When Mabel told her she'd already given it away, that's when Mamaw threw the fit and said, 'Well then, just forget it' and left. Mother lived in New Port Richey then. She certainly hadn't moved to Clearwater yet."

When I insisted that I had been there and that I remembered everything from what Aunt Mabel was wearing to the feel and sound of the gravel and crushed shells in the driveway under my feet to Sheba licking my ears, Mom recalled: "Aunt Mabel did have a dog, didn't she?"

* *

My parents and I visited Aunt Mabel from time to time, but it had to be hush-hush, clandestine in nature. Mamaw knew roughly how long it took for us to make the trip from Huber Heights, Ohio, "The World's Largest Community of All-Brick Homes;" Catonsville, Maryland, a suburb of Baltimore where we lived for several years; or from Kentucky, to the Gulf Coast of Florida, just west of Tampa Bay. If we were running behind Mamaw's carefully estimated time of arrival, there would be questions, and there had better be well-thought-out answers. "There was construction in Valdosta," Mom might offer. Or, "Mother, you've never seen the traffic we saw today."

"You didn't go by and see Mabel, did you?"

"Oh, Mother," Mom would say in a tone that might make someone think Mamaw's question was somehow ludicrous in its mere suggestion.

"Uhmph, Margie Doris, I don't know what you think is so damn special about Mabel. Well, little missy, I'm your mother, not her."

I imagine the mere thought of Mom secretly enjoying Aunt Mabel's company kept Mamaw up nights. Mom was the only thing Mamaw had over childless Mabel, and she was no more willing to share her Margie Doris with Aunt Mabel than an ill-fitting blouse. "Don't you dare . . . let me hear . . . that you've been . . . to see Mabel . . . after the way . . . she's treated me," Mamaw repeatedly instructed us during each of our visits, just that way, through her clenched white dentures.

There were elaborate rules when it came to dealing with

Mamaw, and Mom learned them well. One was to never lie, and I never heard Mom actually lie to Mamaw. There *had* certainly been construction in "The Azalea City" of Valdosta. Now, granted, it might have been residential construction miles from the interstate or a runway extension over at the Moody Air Force Base, but such details were of no concern. And as for the traffic, like Heraclitus stepping into a river, can you see the same traffic twice?

Mabel wasn't alone in her unknown, Mamaw-imposed exile. Mamaw's other sisters—Alice, five years her junior, and Naomi, a dozen years younger—she hadn't talked to either of them in years and had no plans to do so. "Why would I waste time going to see them when they won't come and see me?"

"Mother," Mom would say. "Poor Alice is in a nursing home. You know she can't come and see you."

"Well, then," Mamaw would say, ending the conversation with an emphatic "uhmph."

As for her brothers: "I don't know why my mother had so many children. She was pregnant with Vernon when I had you," she said to Mom. "That's utterly ridiculous—disgusting, if you ask me. Not a one of 'em worth a flat damn."

"Mother," Mom pleaded. "They're your family."

"Uhmph," Mamaw retorted.

* *

Each and every time I saw Mamaw, she said it was probably the last time we'd see each other. After a while, I thought maybe she thought I was going somewhere. The first time I can remember her saying it was in 1967, shortly after Mac died. When Mamaw finally died in October of 2007, I felt compelled to put something down on paper. After weeks of reflection, I penned the following magazine column:

For the first time in one hundred and one Christmases, Mamaw will not be a major part of the festivities. Born in Verona, Kentucky, in 1906, a few days before Christmas, Mamaw—even when living in Florida—was the epicenter of our extended family's plans.

When she visited, which was a rare treat, we would gather in some northern Kentucky restaurant—usually a jumbo buffet—to exchange gifts and catch up with cousins and the cousins of cousins. Relatives would come from three states and hundreds of miles away. (Even Aunt Mabel attended at least one of these gatherings as she was visiting Aunt Naomi for the holidays more than 25 years later, but in my memory they sat on opposite ends of the small room at Ryan's Steakhouse.) When she didn't visit, we would call at an appointed time and take turns bellowing into the phone so that we could be heard over the roar of her television.

"Merry Christmas, Mamaw."

"What?"

"Merry Christmas."

"What?"

"MER-EE CHRIST-MAS!"

"Oh . . . all right. Merry Christmas to you, too."

Every so often someone would ask, "Don't you think Mamaw is lonely all alone down there in Florida?" My dad would say, "Naw, I think she likes her independence."

That was the polite way of saying she didn't want the noise and confusion and clutter that was our Christmas. To her, the thought of paper and ribbons and boxes scattered across the living room was a nightmare. She liked order. Everything has its place and needs to be in it.

When she would send you a gift, she had a place in your house where she knew it should go, and she would check up from time to time to see if you were following her instructions.

Case in point: the brass eagle, purchased from the Home Shopping Network, she sent me for my desk. Its five-foot wing span would look majestic on my four-foot-wide desk. "You know, not many people have an eagle like that one," she would say. She was right.

*Mamaw was a giving, loving person, but she could also be brutally honest. As Pastor Dave said at her graveside service, "Her initials were **B-A-M**, and from what I gather, she was a firecracker."*

My first Mamaw memory centers on "a picture pendant tree" I have in my office. It once stood on the nightstand next to her bed—first in Latonia, Kentucky, and later in New Port Richey and Clearwater, Florida, where she moved after my grandfather, her husband of 42 years, died 41 years ago.

I would sit for hours staring at that tree. I was less than six when I asked her to tell me about the people whose pictures were in it.

"Mamaw," I said, "one of these days you have to tell me about the people."

"What people?" she said.

"The people in the tree. My family. My great-grandfather, the doctor, my aunts, my cousins."

"Are you daft?" she said. "Those are the people who came with the blasted tree."

"Huh?" I thought.

"Yep," she said. Then after a long pause she added, "I like the looks of them better."

Now, back to the long-distance telephone call. First, you have to understand that it was required that two separate presents from each member of the family arrive in Florida prior to Mamaw's birthday, which, as I said, fell several days before Christmas. One of the presents needed to be clearly marked "Birthday" and the other was to be marked "Christmas."

During the call, each of us would take turns asking her if she liked what we had sent. "Oh, yes, it was nice," Mamaw would say. If, however, she didn't like it, it could be emotionally devastating. "What in the world were you thinking?"

That was one of the great things about Mamaw, really. You always knew exactly where you stood, and there was no—absolutely no—chance you might be left guessing.

"When did you start gaining all that weight?"

"Did you think that haircut looked good when you got it?"

"What on earth were you thinking?"

One of the best slices of Mamaw lore came in 1973 at Standiford Field (now the Louisville International Airport). It was Christmas Eve, and Mamaw was coming to town. By chance, WAVE-3 had a camera crew wandering through the airport and magically captured my adorable, blonde, five-year-old niece, Tammie, running up to the gate to greet Mamaw. The two hugged and Mamaw, with her freshly permed pure white hair, hoisted Tammie off her feet. Then,

*looking directly into the camera, she smiled the biggest smile
I ever saw her smile.*

*It was one of those great television moments. So great
that it was re-aired on live broadcasts until the tape wore
out. I'm not kidding, the last time we saw it air during the
Christmas Eve news, Tammie had graduated from high
school.*

*That's the lasting memory I'll keep of Mamaw. Maybe,
if you watch closely and are good, some Christmas Eve
you'll see her, too. "What's wrong with you? Are you daft?"*

*When Mamaw turned 100, we all gathered at the
assisted-living facility she called home for a dinner of gratis
White Castle hamburgers. Who knew that when you turn
100 you can get "sliders" for free?*

*Even then, Mamaw was pretty sharp, although she
sometimes thought my name was either James or Buddy.
She told me that she really liked my family, especially my
son, Chuck, sometimes Chip.*

*   *

While the column was mostly true, it was really only partly
true. I'm not sure how often Mamaw actually said I was daft.
It was a word she used, but I'm unclear on when exactly she
flung that one at me. What she did say, without question, was
that I was afflicted, troubled, a mistake anyone with half a brain
should have known better than to make, and flat-out retarded.
Or when she spoke of me in the third person, looking me square
in the eye: "He just ain't right, Margie. He just ain't right."

The column was the same kind of truth as there being
construction in Valdosta, Georgia, the last stop before the

Florida Welcome Center. The Mamaw in the column is clearly sanitized for your protection. We were taught if you didn't have something nice to say, not to say anything. That meant, in practice, that when Mamaw was around, there was a large vacuum left for her to fill, and she was more than up to the task. Dad could hold his breath under water longer than anyone else in our family. It shouldn't come as a great surprise that, when Mamaw was around, Dad could spend three weeks without uttering more than a half-dozen words. In time, lots of time, I learned to do the same.

When I said that Mamaw's television smile was the biggest I'd ever seen, that was because I seldom saw Mamaw smile other than in the yearly Olan Mills portrait she had taken of herself to give each of us as Christmas presents, and even then it's just a grin, not a smile. I'm nearly positive I never saw her laugh. In the portraits, framed in gold, that still adorn the spare bedroom at Mom's apartment, Mamaw wears an assortment of starched white pantsuits.

Why anyone showed up at the Christmas restaurant gatherings still amazes me more than a decade after the last one was held. "Why would anyone allow someone to talk to them that way?" I can remember asking Mom.

"Well, because they're family," Mom said. "They all understand that's just the way Mamaw is."

"Right," I said. "That's why I'm so surprised they'd even bother."

"Stephen Matthew, she's my mother," Mom would say, using my first and middle names as a cue for me to watch my words. "I know she can be difficult, but she's still my mother."

CHAPTER 5

Agnes Moorehead

I'M NOT QUITE SURE WHEN I first saw Mamaw on television. It could have been a late-night rerun of *Twilight Zone*. It could have been an afternoon showing of the gothic thriller *Hush . . . Hush, Sweet Charlotte*, starring Bette Davis.

More likely than not it was at half past seven some Sunday night on Walt Disney's *Wonderful World of Color*. She was there alongside the lovely, always positive, Hayley Mills in the 1960 classic *Pollyanna*, pretending to be Mrs. Snow, an acidic, neurotic hypochondriac.

I imagined, at some point, everyone in my family to be someone on television—especially those people on the large color set at Mamaw and Mac's Locke Street house. That television was a major piece of living room furniture, housed in a cabinet so grand that it supported future less-grand televisions long after the original's picture tubes had faded away. If not for that set, I wouldn't have known that Lucille Ball had red hair, that Charlie Brown's shirt is yellow (fitting, don't you think?), or that the Green Hornet was, in fact, green. His name should have been a clue, but this is a kid who on some level truly believed that his grandmother was Agnes Moorehead, the iconic Golden Globe- and Emmy Award-winning actress.

The way she pinched her mouth when she spoke. The snarl.

The way the most basic and non-threatening of words, such as "hello," spilled out in venomous form.

The crack of her voice.

The squint.

It was all spot on. The red hair, I assumed, had to be a wig. Mamaw wasn't fooling me. They could call her Agnes all they wanted; I knew her name was Audrey.

Best known as Endora on the 1960s sitcom *Bewitched*, a role which garnered her six Emmy Award nominations, Agnes Moorehead built a 40-year career on bringing Mamaw to radio, stage and screen. Almost without exception, the roles for which Moorehead is best known were characterized as neurotic, selfish, bitchy, nagging, neurotic, treacherous, cantankerous, foul-tempered, neurotic, isolated, fretful, peevish, neurotic, querulous, haughty, arrogant, or neurotic.

Apparently, while Moorehead was quite believable in this type of role, or unfortunately typecast, it apparently wasn't much of a stretch for someone with her credentials.

Dick Sargent, who starred as Endora's hapless mortal son-in-law alongside the oh-so-lovely Elizabeth Montgomery in *Bewitched*, called Moorehead "a tough old bird . . . very self-involved" when he was called for a comment following her death in 1974. He wasn't, obviously, so bewitched after all.

Born in Worcester County, Massachusetts, and raised in St. Louis, Missouri, Agnes Moorehead attended college in Ohio and Wisconsin before entering show business. She claimed to have been born on December 6, 1906, which would have made her 18 days older than Mamaw, if it hadn't been a lie. When she died of uterine cancer, possibly brought on by radiation from a film shot too near a nuclear test site, she was estranged from her family and left her personal effects to the Wisconsin Historical Society. The donation included her professional scripts and her Christmas cards.

CHAPTER 6

Mamaw Returns

MAMAW WAS THE WIDOW OF a railroad engineer nicknamed "Mac" because of his Scottish surname. He was reportedly a descendant of the last Celtic king of Scotland, who ruled from 1040 to 1057 AD and who became the subject and namesake of a well known play by Shakespeare. Thespians worldwide believe it is bad luck to say Mac's ancestor's name in the theatre, so I'll leave it unwritten here.

Mac died of a massive heart attack in May of 1967, in the spring before I turned six. In the story I've been told, Mac was diagnosed with a major blood clot in his leg, and in those days, there was nothing much they could do about it. Mac could take it easy, lay still, and it might take weeks for the clot to reach his heart. When it did, he was told, he was going to have a heart attack, but they had no way to tell how bad it would be. Mac supposedly said he certainly wasn't going to just sit around and wait on an inevitable heart attack, and he walked the halls of the hospital in an effort to increase his circulation and speed its progress. Within 72 hours, the heart attack hit, and within minutes, Mac was gone.

Mamaw and Mac had been married for nearly 42 years, but in the more than four decades I knew Mamaw, I never heard her say anything nice about the man.

I remember him vaguely. Mac smelled of tobacco and Old

Spice aftershave. He always looked like he was about to cry. At the breakfast table, he taught me how to draw snowcaps on mountains. Mac often walked with me up to Johnny's Toys in the center of Latonia to look at the model trains and to the fire station to look at the big red shiny trucks. He sometimes pushed me on the swing in the schoolyard cattycornered from their Locke Street house.

We played dominoes, a game Mac taught me to play while blowing large wispy smoke rings from the cigarettes he rolled with one hand. He could blow one large smoke ring and then shoot Cheerio-sized smoke rings through it. To a five-year-old, it was astonishing that he hadn't yet been invited to appear on Johnny Carson or Jackie Gleason.

"He was always burning holes in his shirts," Mom said. "It drove Mamaw crazy."

Mom meant "drove" figuratively, but to use a well-worn pun, the drive was brief, much shorter than our random visits to unsuspecting relations or the 17 miles between ancient Jerusalem and Jericho, for that matter.

Life with Mamaw had taken its toll on Mac. When I attended the funeral home visitation after the massive heart attack killed him, I didn't recognize Mac as the man in the casket. I had never before seen him smile, even when blowing smoke rings.

"I'd buy him these nice new white dress shirts and had no sooner than brought 'em home and he'd burned a damn black spot on them," she snapped in one of the rare two-party conversations Mamaw and I ever had, still smoking mad about his numerous infractions four decades after they happened. "You do know he went damn mental on me?"

Mental: Mamaw's definition of depression, a condition Mac struggled with for years to the point he volunteered for electro-convulsive therapy (ECT), also known as electroshock, while it was still in its risky infancy. He had probably inherited it, I'd guess from his mother, Maggie, and certainly passed it on to his daughter, some of his grandsons and at least a few of his great-grandchildren.

It was so bad that Mac was on part-time disability at the time of his death, cheating Mamaw, in her less-than-rational estimation, out of hundreds of thousands in Louisville & Nashville Railroad retirement benefits.

"You sure do look a lot like him—especially since you've porked up," Mamaw offered. "You're not quite as fat as your one brother, but you're certainly packing 'em on pretty well yourself, aren't ya? He was always big. He ate the fat instead of the bacon, damned fool."

I never could tell if she meant Mac or my brother Tim, who was once big; I'm guessing she meant Tim, as Mike has never had a weight problem. As for the damn fool, she probably meant Mac, but she easily could have meant Tim. No doubt, Mamaw could have meant me. In many ways, the three of us were interchangeable and of little regard among Mamaw's roster of bit players.

Mamaw had created an ideal world in her head, and by living alone in Florida, little, if anything, could shake her version of reality. In Mamaw's mind, her Margie Doris should have only had one child, so if Mamaw didn't acknowledge Timothy Haystack (Mac's nickname for Tim) or me ("Tiny Britches"), we didn't exist. The problem was, we did exist. Each of our visits with me in tow must have been an irritation to her, a constant, in-your-face reminder of her daughter's blatant defiance.

"Margie Doris, what on earth were you thinking? I certainly thought I taught you better."

* *

In a recent drive-by visit to the Locke Street house Mamaw and Mac shared in Latonia, Kentucky, Mike summed up our family dynamic better than I ever could. "We were raised with a strong belief that we were stars in an unfolding drama in which others were highly interested," Mike said. "Every choice we made, every mistake, was of major importance to a host of great-aunts, uncles, cousins, and especially Mamaw. Looking back, I wonder if some of those aunts and uncles even knew our names."

The lesson was as clear to Mike as it was to me. Disappointing Mamaw was to be avoided at all costs. Nothing could be worse. News of any shortcoming or moral infraction would surely find its way the 897 miles to Clearwater, Florida, and then there would be trouble—an awful, unspeakable wrath. "What are we going to do when Mamaw finds out?" Mom would often say. It was never *if* Mamaw finds out; it was always *when*.

There were no gray areas with Mamaw. There was white, which was good. Then there was black. Speaking back to one's parents, skipping school, or the premeditated slaughter of a busload of innocent children were all the same—especially if it caused her the slightest degree of embarrassment. A violent rape—undetected—was far better than wearing the wrong color socks with your suit—if noticed.

"What on heaven and earth will people think?" I can imagine Mamaw saying. "I have never been so embarrassed. Oh lord, why do things happen to me that just don't happen to other people?"

* *

When I got caught cheating on a high school girlfriend, the girlfriend asked me, when I apologized for the second or third time, if I was sorry because of what I had done or because I'd been caught. I didn't answer her question, thinking it must have been rhetorical in nature. Getting caught was the answer; didn't she know anything? Was she daft?

* *

Until her last couple of years, the years spent in a less-than-desirable nursing home, as if any such-scented place could be desirable, Mamaw always seemed to talk about me and around me, but never actually to me, even when we were face to face. Many times I sat across various breakfast tables from her. "Why on earth did you ever have three children, Margie?" she'd say—looking directly at me—to my mother in another room of the house. "Michael David was a perfectly fine little boy. Having more than one was just asking for trouble. What on earth could you have possibly been thinking? I certainly thought I raised you to know better."

"Oh, Mother," Mom said with her arms shivering just enough to jingle the bracelets that became her trademark fashion statement.

"He isn't going out wearing this, is he? Oh good lord, what on earth will people think?"

"Oh, Mother, he looks fine," Mom said. But I'd be strongly encouraged to change my clothes anyway.

"Uhmph."

Safely out of earshot of Mamaw, Mom attempted to comfort me. "Don't let it get to you—it's just the way she is."

There wasn't much about me as a child that Mamaw liked. For some reason she thought I was going to throw chairs into On Top of the World's swimming pool. Some visiting grandchild from New York or New Jersey whose grandparents lived over in the Colonial Building had apparently done that once, and it was only a matter of time until I did the same or something equally as stupid. She always assumed the worst, but it really wasn't anything I should have taken personally. I certainly was not an isolated target. "Be grateful she doesn't treat you the way she did Tim," Mom often said. "If you think you've got it bad, you have another thing coming, buster. I still shudder at the thought of the things they said to each other."

Tim's lifelong troubles with Mamaw began years before I was born, when he was three, maybe four. Mamaw was having some church ladies over later, and Tim and Mac were watching television in the living room. Mac fell asleep in his tufted wingback chair. Tim climbed under a large gold-upholstered ottoman with white fringe that reached the plush-carpeted floor. He curled up and went to sleep, too. When Mac awoke, he looked around and assumed "Little Timmy" was upstairs with Mamaw. He went outside, got into his green, "stunningly smart," four-door 1951 Buick Super Rivera Sedan, and drove to the store to buy some Bull Durham smoking tobacco, then billed as "the cheapest luxury in the world."

When Mac got back from the store, Mamaw was waiting

for him in the doorway to the backyard. "Where is Timmy?"

When Mac didn't answer, all manner of hell was unleashed. There was screaming. There was cursing. There was gnashing of teeth, or at least, of Efferdent-soaked dentures. "I can imagine she hit Mac, too," Mom added to the story. "I never once saw him hit her, but she'd hit him—especially when she was trying to get his attention."

When Tim awoke several hours later, as the story is told, the house was full of people frantically looking for Mamaw's beloved, missing grandson. In Tim's version, there were at least two dozen church ladies, the pastor's wife, a couple of portly police officers, firefighters, smartly dressed neighbors from up and down the street, and at least one deputized representative from the Covington mayor's office.

Mac was in the garage, alone, sobbing; thinking, at first, that maybe he had accidentally backed out over his tiny grandson and unwittingly dragged the yet-to-be-discovered body through parts of Latonia and Covington. Maybe he hadn't, but he knew without a shred of doubt that he was to blame for Little Timmy's disappearance.

Finally, Tim climbed out from under the ottoman, rubbing his blurry eyes with chubby little fists and asking, "What's going on here?"

Mamaw's reaction: blame and embarrassment.

As Tim recalls it, she said, "How could you do this to me? Why would you make me look so foolish?"

That was in roughly 1954, and other than telling him his hair was too blasted long in 1968 and he was too damned fat in 1988, Tim said he couldn't recall any other direct conversations between him and Mamaw. Somehow, I guess, he's blocked out all the screaming matches they shared, or maybe, as with me, he doesn't classify those verbal assaults as conversations.

* *

"Little missy, you've certainly had enough," Mamaw would say as she approached a total stranger on the sugar-white sands of Clearwater Beach who might have just started turning the slightest tinge of pink. "Little missy, this is a different sun down here, it's a Florida sun, and you need to put something on or go home."

Such interactions could be seen, I guess, as almost benevolent on Mamaw's part, but they'd generally be followed up by something along these lines: "Margie, did you see that poor girl?" with the subject in question still literally feet away and within easy earshot. "Does she think that bathing suit looks good on her? Doesn't she know that everyone can see everything she's got, and there's nothing there anyone, and I mean anyone, would want to see?"

"Mother," Mom would say.

"Uhmph," Mamaw would grunt. "It's the truth."

* *

When I reflect on my two childhood trips to Disney World, both with Mamaw, I am swamped with suppressed laughter and acid reflux. Back in those early days, guests to the Magic Kingdom purchased books of graded tickets. There was the "Seven Adventure Ticket Book" and the "Eleven Adventure Ticket Book," which was an extra dollar. Since our first visit came in June after the park had officially opened the previous

October, it was still a novelty. The winding lines were roughly an hour long each. The "Seven Adventure" was the smarter buy, but the tickets to the most popular rides took the tickets that were scant in the discount book. Through trading at On Top of the World's pool-side clubhouse, the tickets to the run-of-the-mill attractions, such as Cinderella's Golden Carousel, an "A" ticket, were plentiful.

Anything of interest to a 10- or 11-year-old boy, such as the Davy Crockett Explorer Canoes, the Grand Prix Raceway or Mike Fink's Keelboat, was "utterly ridiculous" and completely out of the question.

The guarded "E" ticket included choices such as Pirates of the Caribbean, the Haunted Mansion, the Jungle Cruise, the Hall of Presidents, Twenty-Thousand Leagues Under the Sea and, eventually, the much-anticipated Space Mountain. But no, instead, we would—I kid you not—take a half-dozen turns on "It's A Small World," an air-conditioned, 11-minute boat ride through a multicultural collection of 289 "Audio-Animatronic Doll Figures," each outfitted in clothing and with props reflecting their respective cultures—European, Asian, African, South American children—most of whom Mamaw would have not-so-politely shooed off her lawn anywhere else. "Now, now, Pablo . . . Julio . . . Chewie . . . Chang . . . Paco . . . Mustafa . . . Pedro . . . Get on back to where you belong."

It's appropriate, I guess, that "It's A Small World" was situated smack-dab in the middle of Fantasyland.

It's a world of laughter, a world of tears,
It's a world of hopes; it's a world of fears,

There's so much that we share,
That it's time we're aware,
It's a small world after all.

After the fifth or sixth time through this love maze of diversity, I was truly ready to "go mental" myself.

It's a small world after all,
It's a small world after all,
It's a small world after all,
It's a small, small world.

"Simply lovely," Mamaw said, swaying slightly back and forth in the plastic boat seat. "Why anyone would want to waste a perfectly good ticket on the Haunted Mansion or Space Mountain is beyond me. Utterly, utterly ridiculous. Uhmph."

"But, Mother," Mom said. "Stevie would like to . . ."

"Why are you always giving in to him? I don't know why he should get everything he wants. I never got anything I wanted. Not a thing. Not a damned thing," Mamaw said. "And why on earth does he want a hotdog?"

"He's a child, mother."

"That makes no difference. It's utterly ridiculous."

* *

I never knew Mamaw when she wasn't at odds with someone. I never knew Mom not ready to defend Mamaw's actions, even when they were in obvious conflict with Mom's apparent beliefs. Mom was one person around Mamaw and another who evolved the further we got away from Mamaw's swirling winds. When we lived a few years in Catonsville, Maryland, 967 miles from Mamaw, Mom was the most likely to speak her mind.

"But she wasn't always like you remember," Mom said. "I cut school once because I wanted to go to school with my friend Joyce, who went to a different school. I wrote a note from Mother saying that I was home sick. Well, Miss Rich, who was the dean of women, called and asked if I was feeling better. Mamaw said, 'She's not sick,' and Miss Rich said, 'Well, we have a note from you saying that she is.'"

"Miss Rich gave me seven days of detention, which was spent with the people you didn't really want to associate with, and they had us in a room where everyone could see that you were in there and that you were in trouble. I was so embarrassed.

"When I got home, Mother said she'd gotten a call from Miss Rich and wanted to know what kind of punishment I'd gotten for cutting school and forging a note. When I told her I had seven days of detention, she said, 'That's sounds like a good start.' I would have thought she'd slap me good and scream at me, especially for forging the note, but instead she made me scrub and wax the kitchen floor, which was, to me, as big as a skating rink, for the next seven weeks. It was harsh, and I did it begrudgingly, but it was fair, and I never cut school again."

* *

In Clearwater, which grew from an outpost erected during the Seminole Wars, was a restaurant called the Kapok Tree Inn, because it was built around—you guessed it—a kapok tree that had been imported as a seedling from India in the

1870s. A kapok tree is sacred in Mayan mythology and can grow to be 230 feet tall with a 10-foot trunk. When my wife and I visited Mamaw during our honeymoon in late November 1986, Mamaw alerted us that she had a coupon that we were going to use at the Kapok Tree Inn on Thanksgiving Day. "Yeah, I know, places don't always take coupons on holidays, but this one doesn't say a thing," she told us the day before when we arrived at her condo at On Top of the World. "It doesn't say a thing about not being accepted on holidays. Not a blasted thing."

Mamaw had this conversation with herself more than a half-dozen times that evening and the following morning. "You show me where it says anything about not being accepted on holidays," she said to herself, practicing, I'm sure, for an encounter she expected to be a part of—a heated discussion that she planned to win.

The Kapok Tree billed itself as "serving common food in an uncommon setting." One ad claimed: "When you bring someone to the Kapok Tree, you're saying, 'You are special to me,' but equally, 'I enjoy the finer things in life'."

As a kid I hated the Kapok Tree, and Mamaw, based on our dozens of previous trips, knew it. From the time I was nine, she had been dragging me there at least once during each of our annual visits. It was cheesy and garish, full of faux Italian statues, Victorian fountains, and crystal chandeliers. Outside were formal gardens adorned with more statues and box-cut hedges. I hated the way the place made me feel, and, even more, I hated standing in line. When a restaurant serves more than 4,000 guests a day, ranking in the top 15 grossing restaurants in all of North America, there are going to be lines.

"We have reservations in the Grand Ballroom," Mamaw announced. "It's not every day you get to eat in the Grand Ballroom."

"It sounds lovely," said Kay, my all-too-polite, unsuspecting bride.

"Yes, Mamaw. Simply lovely," I said, echoing Kay's sentiment, but knowing it was going to be simply awful.

The food would be fine. Nothing great, but not bad. The setting would be a hoot, especially for Kay, who had never seen it before, but Mamaw surely would belittle the staff and do something hideously legendary. All I could do was hope and pray she'd be on her best behavior in front of Kay.

"You've never seen Mamaw in action," I tried to explain to Kay later, behind the safety of a closed door, the same door behind which Mom had urged me to change my teenage-appropriate clothes. "She's going to try and use that damn coupon, and they're going to say that coupons cannot be used on holidays, and then the storm will be unleashed."

Why I would take my cheerful bride to Mamaw's house as part of a honeymoon trip would be, I guess, a mystery to most sane people. But, they, these "sane" people, don't understand that it was in the unwritten, but well-understood, rulebook: No visit to the state of Florida could be made without visiting Mamaw. If a trip to Miami (317 miles southeast) or Panama City (414 miles northwest) required a "swing by" to see Mamaw, which they did, the thought of not traveling 164 miles straight up Interstate 75 from Naples, especially less than a week after she had traveled all the way to Louisville for the wedding, was incomprehensible.

"How bad can it be?" Kay asked.

"Oh, it can be bad," I said. "Once when I was a kid, she returned a toaster to a clothing store. When she cut loose, they'd have done anything to get her out of there."

There would be raised voices and demands to see someone in charge. Not only would they accept the damn coupon, in the end they'd be giving her something extra, maybe a seven-day cruise aboard the USS *Kapok Tree*, to make things right. "They don't know who they're messing with, mister," I could just hear her saying to me across the white-linen-covered table. "They're going to damn well wish they'd never tangled with the likes of Audrey."

On that point, she was correct.

To me, the Kapok Tree always looked like an overdone set on *The Lawrence Welk Show*, my least favorite program, but for Mamaw, as for many people of her generation, her favorite program, which I now can trace to her objections to period shows like *The Smothers Brothers Comedy Hour, The Dean Martin Variety Show*, or *Laugh-In*.

She didn't object to the humor. She objected to the guests.

"I am not going to sit and watch them old black things," she would say, which, at the time, could have referred to anyone from Sammy Davis Jr. to Louis Armstrong, Leslie Uggams to Nat King Cole. "They're simply taking over, I tell ya, taking over."

It isn't as if Lawrence Welk didn't have black guests and performers too, but they were somehow different. Honestly, have you seen anyone, black or white, who acted like the people on *Lawrence Welk*? The closest I ever saw in the world outside the television set were the waiters and waitresses at The Kapok Tree, but we'll return to them soon enough.

Keeping up with the many Mamaw rules could be a daunting task.

Any ill-considered comment could unleash the hidden hurricane, brewing just under the surface. Knowing what not to watch on television was among the easiest to navigate. As this was in the mostly black-and-white, three-network era, the viewing options were limited, and she didn't like most of the choices. As I recall, Mamaw liked her daytime soap operas— *The Edge of Night* featured the familiar Cincinnati skyline as seen from northern Kentucky in its opening and closing credits—*The Tonight Show* with Johnny Carson, or at least his opening monologue, and *Hazel* with Shirley Booth. Most everything else fell into ridiculous, utterly ridiculous or utterly-utterly ridiculous categories. *I Dream of Jeannie*: ridiculous. *The Addams Family*: utterly ridiculous. *The Munsters*: utterly-utterly ridiculous. *F-Troop*: "Good Lord, why would anyone with half a brain want to watch that?"

Perry Mason, which Mamaw truly enjoyed, was on its way out as color came in. It was fairly predictable. Even at five I knew Paul Drake, Perry's longtime detective, would uncover some missing puzzle piece. Perry then would present it at the last possible moment, and there would be a zoom in on some guilty-looking stooge. Wait, pause, sound the kettledrum and fade to black.

Of the nearly 300 cases Perry Mason tried, his three losses were in "The Case of the Witless Witness," "The Case of the Deadly Verdict," and "The Case of the Terrified Typist." Even now, as I type my memories of Mamaw, I am terrified.

"What on earth will people think?" I can hear Mamaw say.

*   *

Like me, people of color, if they had only known, shouldn't have felt targeted by Mamaw's wrath. She would have waged war on everyone if she'd only had the time, but a hundred years is not enough. It really was *all* other people she disdained, but with time running short, black ones were just easier to identify. Mamaw wasn't alone among her generation, either. Despite its professed international theme, I would have liked to have seen an Asian or Hispanic or Middle-Easterner or Pacific Islander try to get through the security gates at On Top of the World in 1972.

*   *

When Mamaw first moved to the Sunshine State, she had a white three-bedroom ranch in a neighborhood called Colonial Heights in New Port Richey, Florida, not far from the Pithlachascotee River, which empties into the Gulf of Mexico. Every single house on her street was a one-story and pristine white, as were the people who lived in them. Several people had even replaced the grass with crushed stone, also white. Yes, Mamaw liked things to be white—her cars, her hair, her pantsuits, the sand on her beach, the people in her life.

I couldn't help but think that was part of her reason for disliking her husband. Why she would marry such a dark-skinned man—his complexion a cross between Jackie Gleason and Babe Ruth—was beyond me, especially when his physical (and mental) traits were dominant enough to be passed on to his daughter and grandsons. "Two short days in the sun and you look like you should be on a banana boat," she'd say to

Mom. "People are going to think you're mixed or something."

For my mother, with her penchant for brightly colored plastic bracelets and costume jewelry: "Take a look at yourself. Are you trying to look like Carmen Miranda? Good lord, Margie, people are going to think you're some dirty little gypsy."

* *

Not until her final years in the nursing home did Mamaw use blatant racial slurs. Her brand of racism was more subtle than name calling. When grocery shopping, if given a choice, she would always avoid the checkout lane with a black or Hispanic store clerk, even if it meant standing in a line three times as long.

If, for the sake of this story, she encountered the dumbest of all white people, and they wrongly told her that her order was two dollars and eighty-five cents, she might correct them, but then she'd say, "Poor thing can't count." If, however, a *magna cum laude* graduate of Harvard University who happened to be black correctly told her the total was two dollars and eighty five cents, she'd tell them, "You better check that again, little missy," four or five or six times before she could accept its accuracy. "You gotta watch 'em every second—they're simply taking over."

* *

Mamaw's television was in a converted patio room, which in Florida is called a Florida room. As in most places in 1973, there were the three network stations (ABC, NBC and CBS), a public station, and an independent. The independent is the one that showed cartoons, syndicated programs, and reruns.

In Mamaw's case, the independent station was located in Dunedin, a small town founded by Scottish settlers, less than a half dozen miles away. "You're straining my television set by trying to pull in that damn signal," she would say. "Stop it, stop it right now. Are you daft, or are you simply retarded?"

I remember trying to explain the science behind television. "Mamaw, the signal is sent out, broadcast, from the station's tower, and if it reaches your antenna, you can see it. Your antenna doesn't have the ability to pull in anything from anywhere. It's an antenna, Mamaw, not a fishing pole."

"Uhmph," she muttered. "Stop it. Stop it anyway."

* *

In those disturbingly dark moments when I find myself being less than tolerant or highly judgmental, which happens more often than I'd like to admit, I picture myself sitting alone in Mamaw's bunker-like condominium, secure behind the white stucco walls and guard shack, and I feel ashamed. There I am, surrounded by my things, which include pictures of people I've never met nor care to meet and possessions I have no plans to share.

When visiting Mamaw in the odor-laden nursing home she called home for those last two years, I was embarrassed by the way she treated the nurses and aides. "Put that down, you old black thing," Mamaw snapped. Then turning to us, speaking as if the aide was no longer in the room, similarly to the way she spoke about me to Mom: "What gives them the right to pick over my nice things like a pack of damned coons?" she snapped. "Robbing me blind, I tell ya. They're simply robbing me blind."

"Oh, Mother, what's missing?" Mom asked.

"Well," then after a long denture-gritting pause, "My nice white pantsuit—the one with the gold on the sleeves. Where is it?"

The fact that it had been carted off to either the Goodwill store or the dumpster when Mamaw was moved back from Florida to Kentucky was to remain a deep, dark secret. We, the collective family, could have stepped up and told Mamaw the truth, but no, the truth was seldom the best way to go. How about some half-truths? "Oh, Mother, it could have just got misplaced in the move. I am certain no one has stolen it."

It was true that it *could* have been misplaced, and Mom *was* certain no one had stolen it.

"Uhmph."

More than once, I half-heartedly attempted to sincerely apologize to the nursing home staff for Mamaw's rude behavior, as it reflected poorly on me, which really is the point after all: me. The actual victims of Mamaw's cruel outburst generally countered with the following: "When someone such as your grandmother reaches a certain age, they've earned a little leeway."

"But," I'd argue, "You don't understand. You can't understand. This is not a recent development. *YOU should be appalled. YOU should be outraged.* This isn't old age speaking. *YOU have come face to face with a war criminal, a bigot, a blouse taker. Don't you know she once called me retarded? YOU should stand up to her, and YOU should put her in her place.*"

I might as well have been invisible. These witless victims would continue in her defense, "Miss Audrey is a grand old lady. She's entitled . . ."

She was. Entitled!

She always had been. I don't know if I've mentioned it, but she was legendary for returning items for a full refund at stores that didn't even sell the merchandise she'd purchased. I'm certain that somewhere there is a former Kapok Tree Inn waiter still quaking from that breezy Thanksgiving when, by all that's holy, she did present, and he did accept without question, her blasted coupon. I wouldn't be at all surprised to learn that the waiter covered the difference out of the extravagant tip Miss Audrey's daft grandson may have left just so he and his new bride could avoid the confrontation he stealthily warned the waiter, in advance, would be coming if he didn't accept the blasted coupon without question. Such an action could be, I guess, classified the same as an advanced storm warning, which are issued in specified coastal regions, such as "The Gulf of Mexico's Best Beach," 48 hours in advance, if possible.

* *

One Mamaw memory that survives vividly after more than four and a half decades finds me playing in Mamaw's small backyard on the afternoon of Mac's visitation and funeral at the Connelly Brothers Funeral Home a couple blocks north. The extended family, if you could even then call it such, soon would be coming back to the house on Locke Street, and it was best if I stayed outside and most certainly out of the way.

To appease me, I was given some new Matchbox cars, which each came in their own little paper matchbox. New to my emerging collection were the Fire Pumper, a red Rolls-Royce Silver Shadow, a Dodge Cattle Truck and a vehicle called a

Unimog, which I learned years later is a four-wheel truck still built by Mercedes-Benz.

As I pushed my shiny Matchbox cars along the exposed roots of Mac's beloved catalpa tree, which Mike and I can attest still stands, the feuding neighbor came out of his back door as Mamaw came out of hers. I paused from making the appropriate car, truck and Unimog sounds as the neighbor moved slowly toward the chain-link fence that separated his yard from the driveway the two houses share. As an apparently empathetic five-year-old, I knew, I could sense, that Neighbor was going to offer a kind word of consolation—an olive branch in the midst of the ongoing unpleasantness.

Somewhere along the line, I'd been invited to play in Neighbor's backyard with Neighbor's kids, and I thought Neighbor was funny. He sometimes wore a tattered gray T-shirt with a large hole in it. Neighbor said the hole in his shirt—which was as big as a Frisbee and just as round—was created by a cannon ball that had gone through him while he was fighting in the war. When I relayed the story to Mac and Mamaw, Mac chuckled, but Mamaw "uhmphed" and added the tale to the long list of the utterly ridiculous. "How could you be so stupid as to believe something like that? Are you retarded? You must be retarded. Daft, I tell you. Daft."

That particular afternoon, with me playing in the dirt, before Neighbor reached the fence, Mamaw spun on the heels of her black dress shoes, pointed her thick angry index finger and snapped, "Don't YOU, don't YOU even bother saying anything to me."

"Oh, I'm sorry," Neighbor said. "It's just that I wanted to tell you how sorry I was that HE died," *as opposed to you (for whom I'd feel no remorse)* and he slowly turned and silently returned back inside his dark yellow brick house.

"Uhmph," Mamaw said to no one in particular, certainly not me, her daft grandson fumbling in the dirt with his new Matchbox cars. "I certainly think I put him in his place."

CHAPTER 7

Dad Found

MORE THAN SIX AND A half years passed between Dad's funeral and my phone call to his church to see if, by chance, they still had a copy of the recording of his impromptu Wednesday-night testimonial. I thought all that time that I had a copy of the service in my desk drawer, the safe place that holds many of the random mementos of my life: dance pictures, autographs, newspaper clippings, class photos, and ticket stubs from concerts and basketball, baseball, and football games. There are three fraternity composites and press passes to the NCAA Final Four, the Indianapolis 500, and 17 Kentucky Derbies.

I wrongfully took comfort in knowing it was there, but when I finally found myself in a place emotionally where I could sit down and listen to it, I discovered that what I actually had was an 18-year-old recording of my son's baptism in the same small Lutheran church where Kay and I were married.

It took weeks for Mark, the associate pastor, to find it, but yes, it was there, stored with every other church service from the past decade. I asked if I could borrow it, and once I had it safely in my hands, I had a friend at the local radio station transfer it for me and make copies for Mom and my brothers. Still, I didn't listen to it, not a sentence, not a word.

I returned the original to the church for safekeeping and

then went weeks, months, without listening. Why? Why wouldn't I listen to the stories I had so longed to hear? I guess I was afraid. Not afraid of the stories themselves. Not really afraid of hearing Dad's voice after so many years.

No, I think I was afraid of finding myself in the closing chapter of a book I wasn't ready to end, or maybe I was remembering Dad's rule. "Finish each day and be done with it." Did I really need to dwell on the past to move forward? No. Yes. Maybe? Had I really done all I could do to understand Dad and his impact on me and generations of my family yet unborn? Maybe, just maybe, I was waiting to develop that patience Dad said more than once that I lacked.

As it happened, it was July 28, 2009, the seventh anniversary of Dad's death in the Georgia hospital bed, when I finally sat down next to my own bed and listened to his funeral. It's a good thing I did, because Dad never actually said, "I was born on the banks of the Dismal Swamp," as was so clearly etched in my memory. I would have sworn otherwise. What Dad actually said was, *almost 81 years ago in a little house in southeast Virginia, next to the Dismal Swamp, my mother had a 12-pound baby boy, and that was me.* So my memory was close. He had said Dismal Swamp.

How could I have missed the revelation that Dad had been a 12-pound baby? What an interesting fact to never have known. According to the Centers for Disease Control and Prevention, the average male birth weight in the United States is seven pounds, four ounces. The odds of having a 12-pound baby boy are more than 5,000 to one.

John Wayne, the actor and singular symbol of twentieth-century manliness, supposedly weighed 17 pounds when he was born in a farmhouse in Winterset, Iowa. The largest baby I've ever known personally was Allen Taylor Nall, an 83-year-old gentleman farmer, with whom Dad and I became friends while I was working at a county-seat weekly newspaper in the coalfields of western Kentucky.

Mr. Nall and I worked together on a series of articles to commemorate the 50th anniversary of the 1937 flood, a landmark event in the history of the Ohio and Green river valleys. One evening Mr. Nall, after a homemade dinner featuring his farm-grown lima beans, presented a parable about how small towns such as Calhoun—where Mr. Nall and I lived—had long memories.

He said that, after he graduated from the University of Kentucky in the late 1920s, he returned home to the family farm. He worked. He married. He started a family.

When he was just shy of his 30th birthday, which would have been a few years before the wintery flood, he decided to run in the election for county sheriff. "I couldn't get anyone to take me seriously," he said. "I'd go up to a random farmhouse door and introduce myself. They'd do a double-take and say, 'Allen Nall? Did you say Allen Nall? Well, aren't you that 16-pound baby?'"

Dad heard Mr. Nall's story, too. How Dad's own whopping birth weight didn't come up in the conversation amazes me. It seems like such a birth, especially at home, would have been the crux of family lore. How had his mother endured such an event without doctors and nurses—epidurals and Demerol—is beyond my comprehension. The complications my wife endured with all four of our children would have, if we'd been on the frontier or in a small house near the Dismal Swamp, left me a widower four times over. How Grandma Vest did it alone is another unanswered question. I asked Mom her opinion. "She was a tall woman," Mom said.

As Dad defied the odds in birth, he also did in death. In David Shields' book *The Thing About Life is That One Day You'll Be Dead*, he reports that, in a study of 3,000 American men and women over age 65, people who attended church were half as likely to have strokes as those who never or almost never attended services.

> *The first years of my life we lived kinda in poverty—up*
> *till I was nine or ten, anyway.*

To attest to Dad's poverty, according to Mom, he didn't own a new pair of shoes—other than those issued by the US Navy—until well after they were married. When he graduated from Walton-Verona High School, the home of the Bearcats, his parents couldn't afford the six dollars for a class ring. College, even for the class salutatorian, was certainly out of the question.

Like I said, I never wanted for anything. If I needed it, I got it. If I wanted it, I mostly got it, too. My brothers would say I was a spoiled brat. Not once did I get the traditional speech about "when I was a boy, we were so poor . . ." The fact that he was ever poor was news to me. It was Mom who relayed, upon listening to the tape, more than seven years after Dad's death, that his shoes were hand-me-downs from his well-to-do cousin, Walter, a law school graduate who, as an adult, had been postmaster general for the Commonwealth of Kentucky. Dad's inability to go to college was Mom's major regret, not his.

"He should have gone," Mom said. "He certainly was college material."

"What would he have studied? I asked. "What would he have liked to have been that he wasn't?"

"Oh, I'm not really sure," she said.

It's odd, I suppose, that Dad lived in poverty during the "roaring twenties," a time of abundance in the United States, but not during the Great Depression. I remember asking him once about the Great Depression, which spanned from roughly 1929 until the early 1940s, for a grade-school paper. He said that his family lived so far out in the country that "by the time the Depression got to us, it was over."

In the recorded testimonial, Dad said his family lived in poverty until he was nine or ten, which would be, by my math, until roughly 1931, a year in which 2,500 United States banks failed, *Little Orphan Annie* debuted, and Bonnie and Clyde began their husband-and-wife Texas crime spree.

From research, I know that in January 1931, Dad's family was living outside of Burlington, at the end of Mud Road, which was aptly named because, when Dad and his parents and his three siblings lived there, it was nothing but mud.

It was during that harsh winter of 1931 that Dad's grandfather, Jeremiah Griffith, a 77-year-old widower, died of "renal asthma" while living with his daughter, Clara, my grandmother. When they reached the undertaker via a neighbor's telephone, he said that he couldn't make it to the house and they'd need to get Grandpa out to the main road, which was roughly a mile over mud and snow.

In the story I was told, Clara and the three boys—ages fifteen, nine and seven—strapped Grandpa onto a rock-boat—a bladeless sled—and hauled him out to the highway and back more than once over the course of several days before the undertaker could reach them.

"I remember that he ate balls of salve—you know, like Vicks VapoRub," Dad once told me of his grandfather, Jeremiah. "You know, you do remember something like that."

"I remember that he put a curse on Bill," baby brother Charles said of his grandfather and older brother. "He said Bill was disrespectful. I am sure he was. Weren't we all? I don't remember what the curse was, but it was a good one."

Of his paternal grandfather, Carter Hamilton Vest, "he died before I was born," Dad said. "I don't know much about him."

According to *The History of Kentucky and Kentuckians*, "Carter Hamilton Vest devoted practically his entire active career to the great industry of agriculture and was one of the representative farmers and tobacco growers of Boone County at the time of his death, which occurred in 1907, at which time he was sixty-seven years of age. He was a man of strong mentality and inflexible integrity in all the relations of life, so that he was never denied the unqualified confidence and esteem of his fellow men. He was a staunch adherent of the Democratic Party, and while never ambitious for official preferment, he manifested a lively interest in all that touched the general welfare of the community. He was not a member of any church."

Dad was a Republican, but a less than staunch one. He always said that the way a man votes is between him and the ballot box. During another of the many trips to Florida, Mom and Dad attended Jimmy Carter's church, a Southern

Baptist church in Plains, Georgia, and Dad was thrilled to find himself in President Carter's Sunday School class. He had never, at least until well into his seventies, allowed a political sign of any persuasion in his yard. When I saw the sign, for an incumbent US congresswoman, a Republican, I couldn't help but ask why—why after all these years he had become political? "Well, her campaign office called and asked if they could put a sign in my yard. I told them they couldn't, but that *she* could. I told them I had a few things I wanted to discuss with her, and if she'd come and talk to me personally, *she* could put a sign in the yard. I didn't think she'd show up, but that just goes to show, you never know what's going to happen." What Dad and the congresswoman discussed, I do not know.

As for Dad's Pops, politically he fell between his father and son. He supposedly never voted for an incumbent in any election. The way he saw it was that, by the time any politician rises to the level to be elected, they've made some compromises, so they are, in effect, corrupt. "Give them their turn, but don't let them get too used to things, too entrenched," he reportedly said. "Throw them out as soon as you can and give the next crook (being that they're all crooks) his chance."

In the spring of 1931, the family left Mud Road and moved 20 miles south to a patch of land near Verona that had been in the family since George Vest, a soldier in the Virginia Continental Line, had claimed it for his service in the American Revolution, fighting with General George Rogers Clark in "the wilderness" of what is now Kentucky and Tennessee. George Vest's farm had been divided amongst his daughter and four sons and divided further by subsequent generations over the next century. Charles, the younger brother from the story about the driver's test, still lives on a portion of that original land grant but never knew about how the land first came to be Vest land until I told him about it. Or maybe I just reminded him of something he'd forgotten he knew.

In June 1931, Dad was one of several youngsters informally deputized as part of a roadblock meant to capture the outlaw "Pretty Boy" Floyd. Dad was stationed with his little rabbit rifle behind a wooden pickle barrel at the general store near the Verona crossroads. Floyd had robbed a bank in the neighboring county to the south, but he and his accomplices escaped by a different route under the cover of darkness. "Charles and I sat there most of the afternoon, but nobody, other than the folks we knew, passed by."

While I was in college, a friend of mine was an active member of the Sons of the American Revolution, a genealogical society for men who can trace their family tree to a patriot in the Revolutionary War. When I asked him about the qualifications for joining, he asked me what I knew about my family. I told him I knew my grandfather's name was Charles Byers Vest—I knew that for sure—and my great-grandfather, I thought, was named Carter Hamilton Vest, but that was about all I knew. He said, "I hate to tell you this, but I don't think you'll ever be able to join. There are people who know far more about their families and have worked at it for years and can't get in, so I doubt you could ever do it." I waited for him to say I lacked the patience, but he didn't, although that's the way my psyche must have interpreted it.

I called and asked Dad if he knew anything beyond those scant details, and he said he did not.

My friend, who was making some copies at the store where I worked, happened to have a book of Kentucky wills prior to 1850. In the index there was only one Vest. His name was George, and his will was dated 1845. It was probated in Boone County, the same county where Dad had lived through most of his childhood.

The following Friday, I traveled to Burlington to the same courthouse where Dad and Uncle Charles had taken and failed their driver's test. In the county clerk's office, I met an 80-year-old woman by the name of Fitzgerald who volunteered helping people such as me find the missing pieces of family history. She was quick in her research, and between eight o'clock and lunchtime, she was able to trace my family tree from George (1760-1845) through his eldest son John (1781-1848) and John's second-born son, John Payne Vest (1814-1886), a tavern keeper, to my great-grandfather, Carter Hamilton Vest (1840-1907).

Over the next several years, genealogy became my obsession, and at last count I had connected myself to more than a dozen Revolutionary War soldiers, several Indian fighters, a pair of veterans of the War of 1812, and soldiers on both sides of the Civil War. I found the ancestor who supposedly went mad after being bitten by a rabid dog. I found one man who'd fathered at least 21 children and another who married a week shy of his 97th birthday. When I would present my latest findings to Dad, he would often show interest, but almost as often he would remember that he already knew what I had told him. "Oh, yes, he's the one who was struck by lightning" or "that's right, Carter Hamilton's wife, Miranda Jane—her maiden name was Lewis—yes, did die in a house fire."

"All through the first nine years of my life, I never saw the inside of a church. I saw them buildings around, but I didn't know what they were. One day after school, a nice little lady met me on the street, and she said, 'Would you like to come over to our church for some ice cream and cake?' Well, I was kinda excited. I wanted to see the inside of that building—see what went on in there. To this day, I still want to thank God for sending that little old lady to talk to me. Once I saw the inside of a church, I started seeing the inside of a church more often."

Dad is obviously nervous on the recording. You can hear the staccato beat of his thumbs on the pulpit as he speaks, and there is a tentative chuckle between each of his elevated, nasal statements.

"That's what I want my testimony to be, thanking God for the things He does."

After attending Sunday School and church for several years, two with a devout Sunday School teacher, he was moved during an evening service at the New Bethel Baptist Church in Verona—when he was 12 or 13—to accept Jesus Christ as his personal savior, which is done through a personal confession of faith and baptism, which in the Baptist church is done by immersion, usually in a Baptismal behind the choir loft but sometimes in a nearby creek or stream, just as John the Baptist baptized Jesus in the Jordan River.

"It was a small church and didn't have anybody much to do anything, so when I was 16, they named me Sunday School Director. I can't remember if I did any good or not, but they didn't have anyone to replace me, so we managed."

Sunday School Director would be a job Dad would hold again and again—including at tiny Brookview Baptist Church in Louisville, which he helped start. He was in charge of ordering all materials, arranging and training teachers, and keeping track of attendance. It was a job he would do again at Huber Heights First Baptist Church in Ohio, Catonsville Baptist Church in Maryland, and Parkwood Baptist Church back in Louisville, the church where his funeral was held.

"I got out of school and worked for my dad for a year ..."

That Dad had worked for Pops was news to me. I knew that Uncle Charles had, but other than Mom's faint memory that he might have done some roofing, the year he spent with Pops was never discussed. Why he chose to quit is also unknown. "Don't know anything about it," Mom said.

I couldn't help but wonder if this had been a source of contention. Did Pops want Dad to follow in the family business as Uncle Charles did? Or, being that Dad, a frustrated poet, couldn't drive a nail square, was it was best for him to move on? What hopes did Pops have for his son? Did Pops regret not being able to send him to college?

As for me, I knew that Dad wanted me to be a writer. My only points of departure over which I felt some conflict were my choice to leave the Baptist Church to marry Kay, a born-and-raised Lutheran, and not to "do my duty" and join the military as both of my older brothers had done. Mike was a United States Marine. Tim served in the Army and drove tanks.

As for the church choice, Dad had quoted Genesis. "A son leaves his father and mother . . ." As for the military, Dad said, "You know, Steve, anything worth dying for is worth living for."

". . . and then I went off to the big city. And that might have been a mistake. There's a lot of excitement in the big city. This devout Christian boy kind of forgot about church—there are so many other things to do—and he got involved in things a good Christian boy shouldn't be involved in. He even learned to play cards and roll those little dice."

Why Dad chose to refer to himself in the third person at this point in the story strikes me as curious. For some reason, I find it comforting. He was aware, I take it, that the person he was at 20 was not who he was at 40 or 60. The pool-playing, dice-rolling Harold was a totally different identity. He learned games quickly and well. In years of playing every variety of game, I cannot recall beating him at any—maybe something like Chutes and Ladders, but never games that combined luck with skill. He was a master of strategy. I never knew anyone to beat him at chess.

"I joined the Navy, and those were exciting times."

Dad's ship was commissioned in Boston Harbor on July 30, 1943, during World War II, and retired in 1960. In those 17 years, 748 men served aboard the DD-650, also known as the USS *Caperton*. Named in honor of Admiral William Banks Caperton, it was a 376-foot-long Fletcher-class destroyer, a class known as "The Greyhounds of the Sea."

Two of Dad's shipmates, Earl Hawkins, a Texan who grew up in Mississippi, and Lawrence Zufelt of Bend, Oregon—both nicknamed "Red"—penned diaries of their experiences aboard the USS *Caperton*, which was apparently a clear violation of Navy regulations. For years, Red and Red organized reunions of the surviving shipmates, to which Dad was dutifully invited each year until his death, and to which each year he politely declined.

"Dad, why don't you go? I'd go with you if want."

"I'm not sure that I'd know anyone," he told me. "It's not like we've kept in touch."

According to Mom, there was one friend. She thought his name was Deacon, but that could have been a nickname. She thought maybe he was from New York. They exchanged Christmas cards for a few years, but by the time I came along, that had stopped. I never heard Dad speak of any friends he'd made in the Navy. From reading the Reds' descriptions and the official record, I began to see why. The pieces of the puzzle Dad refused to share began to fall into place. "You dared not get too friendly with anyone," wrote Hawkins. "It was much less emotional to bury someone at sea who was not a close friend."

Among the stories Dad didn't share were how he and his shipmates were tasked with interring the remains of hundreds of charred Marines on the island of Tarawa, the shelling of Satawan and Ponape, the sinking of a cargo ship in Apra

Harbor, and how the USS *Caperton* was used as bait off the coast of Formosa, now known as Taiwan.

Of Tarawa, Hawkins wrote: "The bay was so full of mutilated dead Marines that the sharks were not even hungry." After the battle, the small beaches were so full of bodies that there wasn't enough room to bury both the American and Japanese soldiers. They did the best they could with their compatriots, but burning the Japanese dead became the more efficient measure. "I will never forget the smell of burning flesh," Hawkins wrote.

I heard nothing of the mountains of New Guinea or the bombarding of Kwajalein. I never heard anything about how they rescued the 120 men from the torpedoed USS *Reno*: "By the time we got to her," Hawkins wrote, "some men had started to abandon ship, and they got crushed [by the *Caperton*];" or how the survivors and the 273-man crew weathered constant air attacks and a furious December 1944 typhoon that sank three American destroyers, meaning even more sailors to be pulled out of the water.

Following the typhoon, the ship returned to Pearl Harbor for refitting. Before it returned to combat, Dad was sent to San Diego for several months and then to Norfolk to await his next assignment. He had served 17 months at sea. "Dad knew it was just a matter of time before he was sent back out," Mom said. "That's why we went ahead and got married. There was no telling how much longer the war was going to go."

The one story Dad had told, the one about the kamikaze pilot, was confirmed by both of the Reds' diaries as happening June 19, 1944, off the island of Saipan during the Battle of the Philippine Sea, known as "The Great Marianas Turkey

Shoot." The Japanese lost three aircraft carriers and more than six hundred aircraft in two days. "We could see the pilot," wrote Zufelt of the kamikaze. As for Hawkins, his account said the Japanese Zero—"We called it the red meatball"— tried to land, or crash, on the ship, but at the last moment, after taking too much from the *Caperton's* 20-mm guns, it was forced to ditch into the ocean.

> *"As for church, a few of us sailors gathered from time to time on the fantail of the ship, but I still wasn't doing the things I should have been doing—there were still too many other things to do."*

"When we were not in combat, you could always find a poker game going on around the clock," wrote Hawkins. Other things to do included seeing an exclusive strip show by the famous Gypsy Rose Lee, movies on the fantail, and beer— lots and lots of beer. "We were sent to a rest-and-relaxation camp. The rest was provided in four-man huts. The relaxation consisted of all the booze and green Acme beer we could drink."

Between battles, when the ship could make it to shore, there was more beer waiting on the beach. Each sailor was allotted a six-pack. Wrote Hawkins: "I didn't like beer at the time, and I had plenty of friends willing to buy my six-pack for $10, which was a third of our month's salary."

Following each rescue of a pilot from the USS *Enterprise*, they were rewarded with ice cream, the thing that had first drawn Dad to church and a tradition that continued with us, father and son, after every good baseball, basketball, or softball game and every successful fishing trip. Come to think of it, I think we stopped for ice cream after reeling in the walking catfish.

"Marge and I got married, and pretty soon after that I got out of the Navy . . ."

On August 11, 1945, two days after the atomic bomb was dropped on Nagasaki and four days prior to the Japanese surrender (aboard the USS *Missouri* with the USS *Caperton* pulled up alongside), Mom and Dad were married in the Navy Chapel in Norfolk, Virginia. Mom's parents, Audrey and Mac, rode the Pocahontas, a luxury train on the Norfolk & Western Railway's line, 605 miles for the double-ring ceremony.

En route to Norfolk, Mamaw, Mac and Mom passed through Dad's birthplace, Waverly, named for a series of novels by Sir Walter Scott, the Scottish novelist and poet best known for *Ivanhoe* and *Rob Roy* and the phrase "Oh! What a tangled web we weave, when first we practice to deceive."

"Mother insisted on riding down there with me and being a witness at the ceremony," Mom said. "Mother didn't want anyone thinking Harold and I were living together. I can hear her now: 'I'll not have anyone talking about my daughter that way—that would be just scandalous.'"

From all reports, my grandparents, even then, liked my father well enough from their limited exposure, but my grandfather, Mac, reportedly told Mom if she'd change her mind and go back home to Latonia, he'd teach her how to drive and take her to the circus. He was a funny man, my grandfather. Maybe he knew that being married to Dad for 57 years and raising three sons would be like a circus, and if that was what she wanted, he'd just take her to one.

"It was more like a goat rodeo than a circus," Mom said.

The dynamic of Mom and Dad's relationship was intriguing. Even now, she cackles when she laughs, and Dad seldom more than smirked. You can see it in Dad's freshman class photo at Walton-Verona High School, and you can see it, unchanged, in Olan Mills family portraits taken in 1968, 1973, 1978 and 1983. "It took a lot to get Dad to laugh," Mom said. "When he did, he could make himself cry he was laughing so hard."

As a harmless older man, Dad, as I've said, could be a big flirt. From middle age on, he was known for taking what were called "bird photos." At Clearwater Beach, he would frame up a beautiful close up of a flock of seagulls. Once back home, he would get the film developed and turned into slides. When we watched the slides flashed on our living room wall, we were amazed to find the birds had all taken flight, apparently scared away by some careless bikini-clad young thing who had wandered into Dad's viewfinder.

At least once, I can remember Dad wading through the surf and asking permission to photograph a pair of lovelies. "My 18-year-old son Tim had to stay home this trip," he said. "Would you mind if I took a picture of the two of you so he can see what a great time he missed?"

They ate it up and didn't offer a half-second of hesitation before saying yes.

But from all reports of Dad's younger days, he was shy, quiet, and reserved. "Grandma Vest was that way, too—she just had very little to say," Mom said.

"You know," she said, "I'm pretty sure I was the only girl he ever dated. He liked a girl named Regina, but I don't think she ever knew it. And there was Roberta Tully. He always admired her—they went to school together when he lived in Burlington, and she remembered him years later in Louisville. 'Well, if it isn't Harold Vest.' He said she was the only person in the class that made better grades than he did, but that was okay. They named an elementary school after her."

"We got back into church and started going again every Sunday from then on. That's the beauty of God's love. You can wander far away and you can always come back. He'll always forgive you if only you'll ask."

Church was a big part of who Dad was. He was involved—sometimes as much as five nights a week between deacons' meetings, the visitation committee, and Bible studies. Then there was studying the Sunday School lessons, which he did Saturday nights, after his favorite programs, without fail.

Dad knew his Bible. Once, while I was working at the daily newspaper in Myrtle Beach, South Carolina, there was a conflict about the wages being paid to new hires outpacing the raises given to current employees. I said, "That's just like that story in the Bible," for which I was chastised. "What do you know about the Bible?"

"A little," I said.

I called Dad. "Isn't that right?" I asked.

"Yes, that's Matthew 20," he said. "The owner of a vineyard said to his steward, 'Call the laborers and pay them their wages, beginning with the last, up to the first.' And when those hired about the eleventh hour came, each of them received a denarius. Now when the first came, they thought they would receive more; but each of them also received a denarius. And on receiving it they grumbled at the landholder, saying, 'These last worked only one hour, and you have made them equal to us who have borne the burden of the day and the scorching heat.' But he replied to one of them, 'Friend, I am doing you no wrong; did you not agree with me for the denarius? Take what belongs to you, and go; I choose to give to this last as I give to you. Am I not allowed to do what I choose with that which belongs to me?'"

For a time, I was involved in church too, though not quite on a par with Dad. I even considered possibly going to seminary to become a youth minister. But that was before college and my own discovery of "other things to do." When I started dating Kay, the baby sister of a Lutheran pastor, it was clear that my Baptist days were numbered. I wasn't sure if I'd become a Lutheran, but I knew she wasn't going to become a Baptist.

Dad's response: "It says in the second chapter of *Genesis*: 'A man leaves his father and mother and is joined to his wife.'"

When Kay and I were married, Dad read at the wedding, wearing a tuxedo for the first and only time in his life. He read from *I Corinthians*, the 13th chapter, starting with the fourth verse. He read all of those things that pertain to love: "Love is patient, love is kind. It does not envy, it does not boast, it is not proud. It is not rude, it is not self-seeking . . ."

Dad loved Kay. She was the daughter they'd hoped I'd be. I should have been a Tammie instead of a Stevie. We'd been married for about three years when Dad told me, only half joking, I think, "Marriages don't always last. Mom and I have been fortunate. I hope you know, or you should know, if things don't work out between you and Kay, we're keeping her and you're out."

There are an odd-dozen good old Southern Baptist hymns that find their way into the Lutheran rotation each year. When I attempt to sing "We Shall Gather at the River," *the beau-tee-full river*; "The Old Rugged Cross," *on a hill far awaaay stood an old rugged cross*; or "Are You Washed in the Blood," *in the soul cleansing blooood of the laaamb?*, my endearing wife of nearly a quarter century doesn't hear me. Instead, she hears my father, and if you look closely enough, when I hit that sour note just right, you can physically witness the shiver run up her spine.

> *"About ten years ago, 1st Peter, chapter three, verse fifteen really struck me. 'Be ready always to give an answer to every man about the hope that is within you.' That's not always so easy to do, but I promised I'd try to do that from then on, and then and only then could I say, like the hymn, 'The greatest thing in all my life is serving you.'"*

It was about that time that Dad volunteered and became a regional manager for the Gideons, coordinating Bible deliveries to the hundreds of hotels throughout the greater Louisville area. He did pretty much the same job he did as Sunday School director, only on a much larger, regional scale.

> *"My advice to young people, middle-aged people, is to start younger than I did and do anything that is needed, necessary in the church, and be ready at all times to tell your schoolmates, your co-workers what God has done for you."*

Another example of how my memory of that day was scrambled was that Pastor Phelps spoke after Dad, not before. He commented on how, in time, we would look back on the day and be comforted by the throng that had filled the church and our own ability to reflect, over time, on all that had happened.

"The impact of a man can be measured not by the number of people there to welcome him into the world, but by the number there to say farewell," he began. "By the size of this crowd, it is clear that Harold influenced so many people in so many different ways."

It was in the *Book of Acts* that Barnabas was described as "a good man, full of the Holy Spirit and faith." As Pastor Phelps continued, he explained that Barnabas was known as "the encourager," which he also felt was a fitting example of who Dad was. "Brother Harold enjoyed encouraging people," Pastor said. "If he knew you hadn't been in Sunday School, you could be sure that he would encourage you to attend the following week. Never forceful, but he encouraged others every day, everywhere he went. He didn't speak loudly, never, but he never stopped encouraging. That's what he did. That's who he was."

Pastor Phelps described Dad as a man who was full of joy, peace, and kindness that was best displayed through his faithfulness and his self-control.

Had he heard about Dad's teeth? Had he heard about his lack of self-pity?

"When someone can spend 80 years under the influences of this world and the people who know him best—the people who eat with him every day, work with him every day—still say that he was a good man, and mean it, that says something. I think it's fair to say that, if our city, our state, our country had more men like Brother Harold, we'd be much better off."

How I could have sat through such praise without hearing it is another in a growing list of things beyond my comprehension. How could someone who had known Dad for such a short time capture the spirit of who he was so well? Had he been with us up and down the interstate, at Stuckey's and Cracker Barrel? Had the pastor been there in Benny's kitchen?

* *

It was about a year and a half after Dad's death that Mom asked if I could help her clean out the "O.R.," a room—my former bedroom—where Dad had spent his retirement years working on projects and Mom worked on crafts.

"O.R." stood for OUR Room as opposed to Steve's room, or as I called it, my room. "Who keeps stacking stuff in MY room?" I would often ask upon laundry visits during college, supposing that MY room would remain intact for display in the Smithsonian when I achieved some great measure of success that I was certain I would accomplish.

Calling it Our Room was a declaration of independence, a freedom from parenthood as the youngest of three sons had finally, after oh-so-many years, left the house. I was engaged to be married, and their responsibilities were complete, similar to how Dad on the day following my college graduation—less than 24 hours after I walked across the lawn to shake the college president's hand and take my diploma—went to work, announced his retirement, and gave his 30-day notice.

Sitting at his massive government-surplus desk, where

he did taxes for a herd of senior citizens, coordinated the Bible deliveries for the Gideons, and fiddled with his fantasy baseball and basketball teams, I was surrounded by his accomplishments—his honorable discharge from the US Navy, his 34 years of service to the US Army Corps of Engineers, and his two Congressional citations, for his work on the Mississippi coast in the aftermath of Hurricane Camille and on the Chesapeake Bay following Hurricane Agnes. There was his trophy for coaching a team of 15-year-old boys to the Baptist softball championship. There is another for coaching a team of 17-and-under boys to a triple-overtime victory to capture the city basketball crown. Above those, however, were the photos of his three sons, his seven grandchildren, and his two great-grandchildren.

With the Gideon Bibles gone—now the responsibility of another one of the group's one hundred forty thousand members—Dad's bookshelves were nearly barren. Remaining were a price guide for coin collectors, a copy of a book I wrote in 1993, a dozen worn copies of *Guidepost* magazine, and every single issue of the magazine *Kentucky Monthly* from the first one in September 1998 to the one published the month of Dad's death, in chronological order. Above his desk, in a silver poster frame, hung an aerial photograph of the Grand Canyon, which he said was the most spectacular site he had ever seen. Taped to the glass was a poem he had written about seeing it for the second time. And in the bottom right corner, at eye level, directly in front of his line of sight every time he worked at his computer or picked up his phone, was what I can only suspect was Dad's direction manual—his operating instructions.

There, in seven simple lines written by "Bessie" Anderson Stanley in 1904 for a $250 writing prize—enough to pay off the mortgage on her modest Kansas home—was everything Dad stood for, as complete and chronological as his magazine collection.

He has achieved success who has lived well, laughed often,
*   and loved much;*
Who has enjoyed the trust of pure women, the respect of intel-
*   ligent men and the love of little children;*
Who has filled his niche and accomplished his task;
Who has never lacked appreciation of Earth's beauty or failed
*   to express it;*
Who has left the world better than he found it, Whether an
*   improved poppy, a perfect poem, or a rescued soul;*
Who has always looked for the best in others and given them
*   the best he had;*
Whose life was an inspiration; Whose memory a benediction.

CHAPTER 8

Sand Dollars

I AM AN ILL-SUITED BUSINESSMAN. I have some serious flaws, which show most when we are in negotiations with potential partners. I shy away from confrontation. I have no killer instinct. No thirst for blood. "There goes Stevie, giving away his seashells again," quips Kendall, a sleek, powerful business-woman with an ease for numbers. She is a statistical dynamo, a moneymaker. I am a constant drain on the bottom line, a necessary yet unjustifiable dime-a-dozen editorial expense.

Kendall's quip resonates from a childhood story she once overheard that she firmly believes is the deep-seated root of all my shortcomings—a root so deep and so thick that it would crack most sidewalks, leading to the broken backs of tens of thousands of mothers worldwide.

This story begins when I was nine and living in a gray split-level in Catonsville, Maryland. Mom asked me to get some junk out of the garage. "Do something with it," she said.

I gathered up what I could. I threw a few things away.

The rest I loaded into my red Radio Flyer wagon and set off in search of someone who might appreciate the value in my assortment of treasures: rusted bolts, bottle caps, baseball cards, comic books, some plastic cowboys, Indians and army men. There were some odd-looking rocks, a Mr. Potato Head with some missing parts, The Cootie Game (also missing a few legs and antennae), remnants of my Erector Set. There were five large scallop seashells and five sand dollars the size of IHOP pancakes.

Most everything in the wagon was mine. I guess a case could be made that the seashells and sand dollars were family property.

Mom, Dad and Mamaw had waddled through the surf to a sandbar off Clearwater Beach and pried the sand dollars off the ocean floor with their toes. We then carted them back to Mamaw's house in New Port Richey in a white bucket of saltwater.

Once home, Mamaw took the sand dollars from the bucket and soaked them in Clorox bleach and water until the "creature" was dead and the remains were pristine white. She then sat them on Reynolds' Cut-Rite wax paper sheets in her driveway to dry.

"Now, you know they'll look just perfect in your new house in Maryland, Margie," Mamaw claimed. "Your neighbors will be so envious. You know, it's not everyone who has such beautiful things."

Whether or not Mom had a different opinion was never expressed, but the following spring—after a long and heavy winter—the sand dollars remained on a shelf in our cluttered one-car garage.

With a couple quarters and dimes in a tattered, yellowed Dutch Masters cigar box, I sat out to seek my fortune as a salesman.

I pulled my wagon up one side of Hilltop Avenue and down the other. I skipped Rollingdale and turned right on Rollingfield. At the first house on the right was a pretty blonde lady working in her dormant front yard.

"Now what do you have there?" she said, feigning interest in my wagon full of wares. She wasn't the first, nor last, to pretend for my sake, but then something caught her eye.

"Well, now," the pretty lady said, pointing at the shells and sand dollars. "What, my dear, are you asking for these?"

Not knowing the first thing about supply and demand, merchandising, production, markup, wholesale, retail or price points, I tried my best to think on my entrepreneurial feet. Being, I quickly reasoned, that they were called dollars; they had to be worth at least that much. The shells, being that they were nearly as large and twice as thick, had to be worth every bit as much. Right?

"Sweetie, do you have any change?" the pretty lady asked.

"Not much," I said, shaking the cigar box to make it jingle.

* *

What exactly triggered Mom's rage upon seeing me with a new $10 bill remains a mystery to this day. More than 40 years after the event, I have still not mustered the courage to ask her.

"Where Did You Get That?" Mom roared, pointing to the crisp green bill in my thin little hands, which I guess in 1970 was a denomination worthy of inner-city drug dealers, rural moonshiners and prostitutes, but not a prepubescent peddler of garage debris.

"Well," I said. "I sold some stuff."

"Stuff? What Stuff?"

"From the garage; stuff from the garage."

When exactly Mom drew back her hand and when exactly she brought it in all of its crackling fury across my chubby little face is not clear in my memory. I do remember the sting and the swelling. I remember the tears in her eyes and the recoil from the pain she felt in her hand and wrist as she hit me again and again and again.

Maybe I've jumped the gun here, because Mom wasn't done yelling, and the tears came much later.

"What—Did—You—Sell!?" she bellowed.

"The shells," I said. "The shells on the shelf."

"Mamaw's shells?"

"Yes," I said. "Mamaw's shells."

Was Mom mad that I had sold something that wasn't mine? Was it the thought of Mamaw coming from Florida to Maryland and not finding the shells in their proper place—the envy of the community? "Your son did what?" Mamaw would have surely said. "Are you telling me he traipsed through the neighborhood like a migrant peddler—a dirty little gypsy? Where does he get these ideas? That's utterly ridiculous. Good lord, Margie, what on earth are people going to think?"

Was that it? Shame? Fear? Guilt? I didn't know for sure, and I've never asked.

"How—Could—You?" Mom continued. "Who—Did—You—Sell—Them—To?"

"The nice lady around the corner," I said. "She wanted them for her garden."

Mom's face was as pale as her darkly exotic complexion would allow. She was beside herself; her neck was clenched as she struggled for what to say next.

Had I overcharged the nice lady? Had I sold something

Mom actually wanted? Her unleashed rage was as unyielding as Jesus driving the moneychangers from the temple. I was, I could see, as despicable as the Roman soldiers who cast lots for Christ's clothes at the foot of the cross.

The sand dollar represents the life of Jesus. A Southern Baptist minister said it's obvious to anyone who just looks hard enough. The five-pointed star represents the Star of Bethlehem. There's an Easter lily and a Poinsettia hidden in its design. The five holes represent the nails driven through Jesus' hands and feet and the soldier's spear that pierced his side. Breaking open a sand dollar reveals five small doves, an obvious sign of God's forgiveness and our salvation.

Mom's open-handed smacks rattled my teeth and rippled through me like a tsunami, reverberating in my fingers and toes.

"You—March—Yourself—Right—Back—Up—There—Mister—And—Give—That—Nice—Lady—Her—Money—Back," Mom bellowed. "What—On—Earth—Will—People—Think?"

Which people? What had I done that was so wrong? What law had I broken? Which line had I crossed? Whatever lesson I should have learned from the experience was lost on me. As I've said, I never asked.

But I did march myself back up Hilltop and right on Rollingfield, stomping on each and every sidewalk crack I could find. By the time I returned to 13 North Hilltop Road, I had traversed the gray concrete sidewalks of Rollingbrook, Brookside and Rollingwood, too. I had broken my mother's back hundreds of times, and she didn't even know it.

"Did you give the lady her money back?" Mom, from

another room, asked when she heard me slink into the house through the garage.

"Yes, ma'am," I said.

*   *

"But, what about the seashells?" Kendall asked the first time she heard the story.

"What about them?" I said.

"When you gave the nice lady her money back, did you get your shells?"

"No," I said. "They were already in her garden."

"But they were yours."

"Yeah, I guess."

I could imagine Kendall wanted to draw her own arm back and slap some sense into me. I can imagine I'd flinch. But she lets it go. Or I should say that she places it safely back into her crowded arsenal to be dispensed again and again when my fiscal shortcomings—as they so often seem to do—show themselves.

"I'm sure a psychoanalyst would have a field day with that story," Kendall says.

"Yeah, I'm sure they probably would," I say.

More than once I've left such debates of my obvious flaws to walk off my frustration. The office park where our magazine is located, fortunately, at least for Kendall, a mother of two, has no sidewalks.

CHAPTER 9

Dissecting Frogs

TWO OF MY NIECES—TAMMIE AND Amanda—are blue-eyed blondes like their mother and my father. The other, Lynette, is exotically dark like her father—my brother, Mike—my mother, and me. Once, while visiting my mother—her grand-mother—Amanda, then roughly four, announced that she and those in the family who looked like her were "angels" and should be referred to forevermore as such.

"What about us who don't?" Mom asked.

After a long, thoughtful silence, Amanda said, "Frogs. You're frogs."

* *

The French are often called "frogs," and they don't like it much.

Historians say it's because they eat frog legs. Another theory is that the Emperor Charlemagne's war banner boasted three toads, and the Welsh and English weren't bright enough to know the difference. One suggested reason is that the Fleur de Lis—also Louisville's symbol—is, if you really use your imagination, sort of frog shaped. Another theory is that Queen Elizabeth I nicknamed Francois, the French Duke of Anjou, "frog" after he presented her with a frog-shaped earring during his unsuccessful courtship of 1579 A.D., and eventually the disparaging term grew to include all French people.

* *

I'm not sure I know the difference between a toad and a frog.

* *

In Kentucky, the Bluegrass State, there are more than 20 varieties of toads and frogs, including the eastern spadefoot, the northern and southern leopard frog, the cricket frog, Fowler's toad, the mountain and upland chorus frogs, the pickerel, the barking and bird-voiced tree frogs, and the spring peeper.

* *

Following Amanda's declaration that her Granny, my mother, was a frog (which you need to understand is a memorable moment in Vest family lore), everyone started giving Mom frog-themed gifts. Like with Queen Elizabeth I, it started with jewelry.

* *

You may remember that my mother's aunt, Mabel, made ceramics. She had her own kiln and in the rural area surrounding Eureka, Fort McCoy and Ocala, Florida, she was the foremost authority on all things ceramic. Aunt Mabel's classes were taught in an outbuilding on her property that had been used as a community building by workers constructing the Eureka dam and Rodman Reservoir on the Ocklawaha River, a section of what was to be a canal across northern Florida, connecting the Atlantic with the Gulf of Mexico, until a halt in funding stopped construction several hundred yards from Aunt Mabel's front door.

* *

My earliest memory of frogs was shooting them with red-headed Mark Kern's new Daisy BB rifle in an overgrown drainage ditch, a creek that ran through our subdivision in Huber Heights, Ohio.

My father said purposely killing any living creature—even a frog—that I was not prepared to eat was sinful. It never happened again.

* *

In order to pass freshman biology in high school, we were required to dissect a frog. I don't know how I managed to pass the class without doing it.

* *

Aunt Mabel's house sat across the Ocklawaha River from the Ocala National Forest, northeast of Silver Springs. Her husband, Gus, had bought the swamp land for his hunting and fishing retreat. He liked to hunt. He liked to fish. After his death, Aunt Mabel, who didn't like to hunt or fish, sold and donated part of the land to the federal government for the barge canal project. The rest she turned into a housing development—a trailer park with two dozen concrete pads—for the construction workers, making a small mint in the process.

* *

Kermit the Frog first appeared on *Sesame Street* on November 10, 1969. I was eight at the time of his debut, which would mean I was probably a little too old to watch *Sesame Street*, but I enjoyed the show just the same. One of my first car dates came 11 years later when I took Wendy to see Kermit in *The Muppet Movie*.

I was so eager to impress Wendy on our one and only date that I borrowed a classmate's red Firebird and claimed it to be my own. Ashamed to drive either Dad's Country Squire station wagon or the recently acquired Cutlass Supreme Oldsmobile, I concocted the fraud, which I could not replicate, so a second date never materialized. "If she's going to judge you by the car you drive, maybe she's not the girl for you," said Dad, who certainly knew the girl better than he knew me.

Who was I to be judged on my own merits? I clearly knew, as would anyone paying attention, I had none. It would be fair to say I was compensating for something, but for what, I certainly had no clue.

* *

During one of our covert visits to Aunt Mabel's, I struck up a friendship with one of the construction workers' sons. I think his name was Jeff. To have something to do, we had a contest to see which of us could catch the most frogs and toads. Each of us had a two-gallon plastic bucket. We each filled it to the brim.

Since we'd had so much fun catching one bucket, we wanted to do it again, but Jeff and I needed somewhere to store our first round of frogs while we went in search of round two.

*   *

Florida is home to 27 species of frogs, but only 16 varieties live in the central region in which Aunt Mabel resided. The terrestrial variety, those which can be found on the sandy soil and hiding beneath plants and logs, include the cane toad, the southern toad, the oak toad and the eastern spadefoot. Non-native interlopers include the greenhouse frog, the little grass frog, the southern chorus frog, and the gopher frog.

*   *

Florida classifies three kinds of migratory residents—snowbirds, snowflakes, and frogs. Snowbirds are those who buy property in Florida and spend their winters there. Snow-flakes are renters who winter in various locations across the state. Frogs are former snowbirds who opt to stay in the Sunshine State until they croak.

*   *

Jeremiah was a bullfrog.
He was also Dad's grandfather and my great-grandfather.

*   *

The heavy wooden back door to Aunt Mabel's house had a storm door with three square panels. The bottom panel was metal—probably dimpled aluminum. The center panel was Plexiglas. The upper panel held a screen, but during that visit, the screen was missing.

Why we chose the airspace between the storm door and Aunt Mabel's backdoor as the repository for our frogs is a mystery to me now, but I'm sure it appeared totally logical to a pair of nine- or ten-year-old boys.

*   *

In Scotland, dating to the early Middle Ages, frogs were considered lucky, which is why stone garden frogs are often given as housewarming gifts.

*   *

Jeff and I filled three more buckets each before the frogs and toads were clearly visible through the bottom half of the storm door's Plexiglas panel. The frogs squirmed, crawled and jumped against the Plexiglas. Lit by the back porch light, the scene looked, if you can imagine, like a slimy green ant farm. Jeff and I giggled, squealed or hooted, which for some reason prompted Aunt Mabel to open the door from the inside, a possibility neither of us had considered.

*   *

There are more than five thousand species of frogs, and they are a prominent feature in all forms of folklore worldwide.

*   *

Molly once counted more than 800 frogs in Mom's two-bedroom luxury retirement suite. Mom has a frog clock in her guest bathroom with a different croak for each hour. One o'clock, the spring peeper. Two o'clock, the American toad. Three o'clock, the granular poison-dart frog. Four o'clock, the green frog. Five o'clock, the gray tree frog. Six o'clock, the pickerel. Seven o'clock, the coqui. Eight o'clock, the wood frog. Nine o'clock, the red-eyed tree frog. Ten o'clock, Couch's spade-foot toad. Eleven o'clock, the Pacific tree frog. Twelve o'clock, the bullfrog.

Mom has frog pillows and blankets. She has a frog-shaped flower pot. There is a frog oven mitt, pot holders, rugs and mugs. Door stoppers. Lamps. Dishes. Cups. Mom has a frog-adorned shower curtain and a matching toilet seat cover. Soap dish. Towels. She has a statue of a bullfrog holding a sign that reads "Caution, Frog Crossing" and another that says "Beware of guard frog." Standing frogs. Sitting frogs. Frogs that sing. Frogs that dance. Mom has a frog snow globe, salt-and-pepper shakers and drink glasses. The light-switch covers boast frogs.

* *

The individual number of frogs unleashed into Aunt Mabel's small house on the muddy banks of the Ocklawaha River was not recorded, but it's safe to say our cache of nearly 16 gallons of frogs was substantial—more than the ornamental kind found in Mom's apartment, which is, to say the least, overwhelming.

"Oh good lord, Margie," I can remember Aunt Mabel, sounding a little like Mamaw, moaning in astonishment as she swept the last of the frogs out the kitchen door. "What on earth was your boy thinking?"

* *

In medieval Europe, the frog was the symbol of the devil.

* *

Years later—nearly two decades later—I took Kay to visit Aunt Mabel, who by that time had sold the rest of her swamp land and moved into a three-bedroom condominium in nearby Ocala. To avoid being bothered by potentially noisy neighbors, she also bought the matching condo above her own and used it to store, among other things, her ceramic alligators, flamingos and frogs.

Despite the overwhelming size or Aunt Mabel's new two-floor domicile, six furnished bedrooms, she was quick to suggest several nice hotels in the greater Ocala area, the original "Kingdom of the Sun," in which for me to stay.

Mom for the Prosecution

IN THE 24 MONTHS SINCE I first started putting these particular words on paper, Margie Doris, my mother, has spent more
than 150 days in the hospital and another 30 in various reha-
bilitation centers following a botched colonoscopy that has left
her a physically diminished woman with a highly functioning
mental capacity and a selective memory.

In that span of hospital and rehab stays, Mom died three
times—actually coded—and the extended family has been
called to her deathbed a half-dozen times only to see her mirac-
ulously bounce back and persevere. The routine procedure
that caused her health to spiral downward predates Mamaw's
death, which mercifully arrived shy of Mamaw's 101st birthday.

With all of the days confined to treatment facilities, Mom
and I have had scads of time between blood-pressure checks to
hash over my childhood and to determine which memories are
valid and which ones are suspect. Regarding the recollections
of my father, she claims I portrayed him flawlessly, though
a couple of geographic locations, in Alabama and Georgia,
could possibly be wrong. As for Mamaw, I didn't have much,
if anything, right.

Our biggest contention is over the story you may remember,
in which Mamaw and her sister Mabel exchange words—well,
at least Mamaw did—in the driveway of Aunt Mabel's home

in Eureka, Florida. Mom argues that the showdown never happened, or, at least, not the way I remember it. She claims that the sisters' stormy relationship came to a head over a team of white ceramic reindeer pulling Santa in his sleigh, which Mabel made and Mamaw originally rejected, prompting Mabel to give it to some insignificant—at least in Mamaw's opinion—neighbor.

When I argue that my memory is crystal clear and that it involved Aunt Mabel not dropping everything she was doing the moment we arrived, she claims that I couldn't possibly remember it, because we were forbidden from visiting Aunt Mabel long before I was born. No, no, I claim. I was there when the edict came down, forbidding us from visiting Aunt Mabel ever again. But maybe Mabel was purged from the family more than once. As hard as it would be to fathom, maybe Mamaw had stomped off in a huff before. Actually, no, that wouldn't be at all difficult to believe. "Well then. Uhmpf. If you don't have time for your own sister, just forget it."

Part of the reason I believe I remember the incident so clearly was that it was linked to a secret visit to Aunt Mabel's. The process of concealing something makes it much more vivid to the keeper. Why did Aunt Mabel's dog Sheba come down the driveway to greet me as a friend instead of barking and growling at me like a stranger? Maybe because we— Mom, Dad, and I—had been at Aunt Mabel's house just days before.

We had gone into Silver Springs in Aunt Mabel's brand new convertible, a turquoise Oldsmobile Delta 88, for a late lunch. On the way, Aunt Mabel hit a large American White Pelican that had waddled up out of the marsh. The bird was in the third or fourth gyration of its long, broad white wings when its large, heavy body struck the right side of the hood and then a nanosecond later, the large red pouched bill clipped the windshield, just above my buzz-cut head. The resulting explosion created a shower of pelican parts, blood and feathers, covering the faces and new sporty vacation clothes of my parents, riding in the back seat.

Aunt Mabel hadn't seen the majestic, yet awkward-looking, waterfowl. I had seen the bird, but for once I couldn't say anything. I watched speechlessly as Aunt Mabel's new ride bore down on the floundering fowl.

Aunt Mabel was driving left-handedly and well above the speed limit. Her tanned right arm was thrown over the leather seat between us, and she was turned and engaged in an animated conversation with my parents when they abruptly transformed into the Kennedys in the back of Texas Governor John Connally's limousine in Dallas on that sunny day in late November 1963. "I'll never forget it . . . It was so quick and so short, so potent," Nellie Connally, the First Lady of Texas, recalled in a 2003 interview with the Associated Press. In remembering the 40th anniversary of the president's assassination, she said, "It's the image of yellow roses and red roses and blood all over the car . . . all over us."

My image from 1969 is the same: potent—except, well, it was bird guts and feathers instead of blood and roses.

"Oh, good lord," Aunt Mabel said. "You two should see yourselves. You've never seen such a mess. Good lord."

Once we got Mom and Dad back to Aunt Mabel's house and cleaned up, Mom delivered the standard lecture about "not a single, solitary word about any of this can ever get back to Mamaw." Not a word about the pelican; how much you enjoyed your lunch; or how Sheba finally warmed up once she got used to you being around. Mom's message was clear: Mamaw couldn't know that we had been to see Aunt Mabel.

We didn't visit Aunt Mabel all that often, less than a dozen times. It's just that those memories—hermetically sealed in secrecy—are still there, trying, like that poor hapless pelican, to take flight.

*   *

Amanda likes to believe Mom's admiration for frogs began with her witty childhood comment in which she labeled Mom as a frog, but Mom had frogs—ceramic ones—crafted by Aunt Mabel, years, more than two decades, before Amanda was even born. The first frogs, I assume, were an inside joke between the two of them about the day Aunt Mabel's daft nephew unleashed Moses' second plague upon the Egyptians into her kitchen.

> *. . . frogs will come up and go into your house and into your bedroom and onto your bed, and . . . into your ovens and into your kneading bowls.*

Mamaw never heard a single word about the frog incident, which should stand as proof that I can, when absolutely necessary, keep my mouth shut. It also gives credence to my memory of the disputed driveway showdown.

Jeff, my frog-collecting partner, lived on Aunt Mabel's property only because his father was a part of the team constructing the Cross-Florida Barge Canal.

The US Army Corps of Engineers, Dad's employer for more than three decades, began construction of the Cross-Florida Barge Canal in February 1964, but the section near Aunt Mabel's house wasn't underway until after the H.H. Buckman Lock, just upstream, was opened on December 14, 1968. We—Mom, Dad, Mamaw, and I—attended the dedication ceremony and I sat, in a most-uncomfortable little suit, with Aunt Mabel on the raised plywood platform. I wore a stiff dress shirt that pinched my neck. Mom and I agree on this point, and it is documented. Not the shirt part, the dedication part. The workers and their families arrived soon after and remained until construction was halted by President Richard Nixon on January 19, 1971, despite the $74 million that had, by then, been spent on land acquisition, to people like Aunt Mabel, and to construction workers, such as Jeff's father.

In my memory of the great driveway showdown, the trailers were gone from Aunt Mabel's property, but if the frog incident and another visit, during which Jeff and I used a post-hole digger in an thwarted attempt to visit China, only to hit water, happened before the final confrontation, why was it so important that those events, too, be kept secret? Could it possibly be that the feud was ongoing and had little, if anything, to do with the team of white ceramic reindeer pulling Santa in his sleigh?

*   *

Mom loves to tell a tale about the nearly four-year-old me. That's when Mike joined the Marines, Dad was away on an Army Corps of Engineers project and Tim was gone—in the day, at school; at night, working and partying.

"Daddy *leeb* me. Mike *leeb* me. Timmy *leeb* me," I said. "*Pleebe*, Mommy, don't you *leeb* me, too."

From that day in 1965 until the day I abruptly left home more than 15 years later, every moment not spent at church or in school was spent with Mom. I went with her when she went shopping. I went with her to the post office. I went with her to the beauty shop. I went with her when she visited with the other ladies from church.

"It was like we went steady for a very long time," Mom said, validating my memory of my childhood, as I have scant childhood or adolescent memories that do not include Mom. "You wanted it that way. You oh-so-hated being alone." I still do.

I liked the post office much more than the beauty shop, but I also enjoyed some of the visits between housewives. Some of Mom's friends had kids I could play with. One of the ladies had a daughter who enjoyed the two of us taking turns tying each other to her bed. Entire afternoons were spent with her tying me down, leaving me in the dark, and then rescuing me, and vice versa. The easily excitable five-year-old Stevie, buried deep inside the staid adult version, can't help but wonder from time to time whatever happened to her.

* *

Some say Mom coddled me. My brothers, I'm sure, would say I was outright spoiled. Others, if given a chance to think about it, might say Mom dutifully sheltered me like a mother protecting her child from an oncoming tropical storm. She bolstered me, sure, but in many ways, more than anything else, Mom wounded me.

Those who said she spoiled me are correct. I cannot remember a single time I did anything for myself as a child. Mom did everything for me. She set out my clothes. She made my bed. She tied my shoes.

For every lunch, from age four to seven, I had a butter-and-jelly sandwich on white Wonder Bread, fortified with vitamins and minerals. Did you know that's where they came up with the title for the 1980s coming-of-age television show, *The Wonder Years?* It's drawn on the notion that Wonder Bread will nourish children through adolescence.

From age seven to seventeen, I had a peanut butter-and-jelly sandwich on white Wonder Bread. Each sandwich was made with first Peter Pan and later Jif peanut butter (smooth, not crunchy) and Welch's grape jelly. The sandwich was then cut diagonally and carefully wrapped in wax paper. It didn't matter if the sandwich was destined for a brown paper bag to be toted to school on the bus, or for me while I was sitting in front of the television less than 10 feet away. Some days—most days—I'd have a sandwich for both.

Other children had more exotic-sounding sandwiches, such as grilled cheese or marshmallow cream, but if I knew anything, it was that lunch was not intended to be an adventure.

Each of the estimated three thousand, three hundred and eighty sandwiches was cut just so and wrapped in non-stick Reynolds Cut-Rite wax paper. "Here you go, honey," she'd say. "It's just like you like it."

Rounding out each anticipated midday meal were 12 Mike-Sells or Charles Chips potato chips, three Oreo cookies and a cold glass of milk, served to me on a TV tray. Mom knew better than to try to sneak Hydrox or, heaven forbid, Lance sandwich cookies into my brown-paper lunch bag. Even before I could read, I knew the difference, and the wrath of the Oreo-deprived or deceived can be unnerving.

"Anything else, honey?" Mom asked as I reclined in "my chair," speechlessly glued to afternoon reruns of *Gilligan's Island*, *The Munsters*, and *Speed Racer*.

* *

By the time I came along, Mom had honed her parenting skills. She'd hoped to practice them on the daughter she'd always wanted, but I'd have to do. She had freed herself from most, but not all, of the abuses passed on from her mother and absent and damaged father.

Mom enjoyed using the leather belt and knew how to wield it like a lion tamer. She never struck a blow on the buttocks, knowing that didn't hurt as bad as the back of the thighs, just above the knee. She used precision when laying leather to flesh.

While Mom enjoys the story of the clingy nearly four-year-old, she's not so fond of the tale that follows. It takes place less than a year later in that now strange world where mothers, for the most part, stayed home, and children, for the most part, played in the free-range outdoors.

Jodi, my companion in my first whirlwind adventure, was a short-haired blonde who claimed, with all her might, to be a boy. I'm guessing we were at least four but no more than five years old. Mom later confirmed that fact to be true. We *were* less than five. Jodi hit like a boy. No doubt about that. "No, you can't kiss me. I'm a boy, and boys only kiss girls," Jodi would say.

With that issue out of the way, we did all the things that

boys do. Decked out in Army surplus helmets with green netting and camouflage jackets, toting ammo boxes and clip belts, we had all-day dirt-clod fights. We played Hot Wheels and GI Joes and climbed stuff—lots of stuff—trees, hills, and TV antennas.

Jodi lived in a two-story yellow brick house with white shutters, six houses up the curb-lined street from my family's L-shaped ranch on the outer edge of a developing subdivision aptly dubbed "America's largest community of all-brick homes."

Beyond our immaculate yards of green velvet sod was "the wilderness," which in our minds was—in the mid-1960s—as expansive and dangerously unknown as the American West was to William Clark and Meriwether Lewis in August 1803.

The dirt-clod fights had taken us to the fringe, but never had anyone we knew ventured out of sight of the two dozen brick homes on the north side of Larcomb Drive. "There's a creek over that way," Jodi told me. "What's past that, who knows?"

In my reconstruction of the weekday adventure, one morning we were playing with my plastic cowboys and Indians in my parents' one-car garage. Jodi and I then played a game or two of Cootie, in the red and yellow box, and Mr. Potato Head before getting into Tim's discarded Scouting gear.

Without much discussion, we silently began gathering must-have provisions—a package of peanut butter crackers, some M&Ms, a broken transistor radio, a plastic hunting knife and my bow and arrow from Ghost Town in the Sky. Jodi and I crammed what we could into a daypack and filled the canvas-covered canteen with lukewarm water from the green garden hose.

We then stepped boldly into the woods and disappeared.

For the first hour or so, we could still see the light-gray roof shingles of Jodi's two-story house. Even from the creek, which was right where Jodi said it would be, we could see the Worleys' television antenna through the brush and shoulder-high scuffs of brown grass. The Worleys lived next to the house of Jodi's neighbor, Buzzy, a dangerously squirrelly kid who, even at seven, smoked and claimed to have a functioning machine gun in his attic that his father had brought home from Korea.

I'm not sure who urged whom to venture past the creek. Maybe neither of us did. Perhaps each of us was simply bolstered in knowing the other was there. Hours passed. We devoured the M&Ms first. Then the Lance peanut-butter crackers. By our estimates, we were 20 to 30 miles from home. The sun, which was still rising when we left home, was now setting. It was a cool day with a nice breeze, but we had ventured too far and both knew it. We were certain that we might never see our neighborhood again. No one would know where to begin looking for us. Sure, they'd try, but once the dogs lost our scent, we'd fade into memory.

Why hadn't we left a note? Well, maybe because neither of us knew how to read nor write.

As Jodi and I turned again toward what we thought was home, I refused to cry. I had to remain strong for Jodi because she was a girl, after all, even if she wouldn't admit it. "I'll get you home; don't worry," I said, boldly. "There's no need to be afraid."

More hours passed. Vultures circled high above "the wilderness." We were certain the police had been called. Maybe the National Guard. Our dads probably had to leave work early at Wright-Patterson Air Force Base and were none too pleased. Maybe they thought Jodi and I had drowned. Maybe they thought we had been kidnapped by hobos or stolen by the gypsies Mamaw was always talking about.

When Jodi and I emerged from the woods, we were in another neighborhood—slightly older but identical to our own. We had, like Christopher Columbus, discovered a new world.

Once I had gathered my wits, I recognized one of these foreign houses as belonging to Elizabeth, one of mom's friends. Elizabeth went to our church, sang in the choir and taught Sunday School. Elizabeth lived near the Thompsons, which was on the other side of town. In my adolescent estimation, Elizabeth's house was some two hours, by car, from our house. How on earth had Jodi and I ended up here? "I know this house, Jodi. You can relax. You're going to be OK."

We rushed to the sliding glass door and knocked. I told Elizabeth in rushed detail how I had saved Jodi from a perilous fate, involving snakes and coyotes, hobos and gypsies, and how I had done the responsible thing by bringing Jodi to safety. "I saved her," I said.

"Her?" Jodi groaned. "I'm a boy."

Elizabeth offered us freshly baked chocolate chip cookies and cold milk while calling Mom and curiously engaging her in a game of guess-who-I-have-in-my-kitchen over her moss-green wall phone.

"WHAT?" I could hear Mom scream. "I'LL TAN HIS LITTLE HIDE!"

"No, Mom, let me do it," I could hear one of my brothers,

probably Tim, offer in the background. "Let me teach the little squirt a lesson." Within seconds, the white 1961 Ford Fairlane was in the driveway, and Jodi and I were whisked away, me by the ear, from Elizabeth's cookies and milk, neither of which we were able to finish. "When I Get You Home, Mister . . ." Mom continued to rage.

We dropped Jodi off at her house. Minutes later I met the belt in the garage where our adventure had begun. As the brown leather belt cracked across the backs of my thighs, I tried my best to explain that I was a hero, a savior, a good-deed doer. "You'll learn not to do that ever again," my brother offered.

Within weeks, Jodi and her Air Force family moved to Turkey's Incirlik Air Base with her still claiming to be a boy.

Looking back today, I know the beating wasn't nearly as severe as my memory longs for it to be. I know that the true distance between our house and Elizabeth's was, at most, four-tenths of a mile. Jodi and I had been gone for most of the day, true, but there were no calls to the Dayton Police Department or the National Guard. There was no government-led search party. If we'd have been able to find our way home before the street lights had come on, Jodi and I, even as wee preschoolers, wouldn't have even been missed.

* *

While Mamaw bore a striking resemblance to Agnes Moorehead, Mom, as a younger woman, looked and sounded like a prettier version of Margaret Hamilton, best known as the Wicked Witch of the West in the 1939 classic, *The Wizard of Oz*. Her hair was jet black, and both her voice and laugh have that witchy cackle. Years before I was born, a curtain rod fell, breaking her nose, giving it that much-needed witch-like crook.

With the exception of Buzzy, all the kids on Larcomb Drive, where we lived until I was nine, believed Mom was a witch and only reluctantly would come into our yard to play. She could and would, upon request, launch into Margaret Hamilton's awful witch laugh and scare the shit out of us all. "I'll get you, my pretty . . . and your little dog, too!"

Those precious moments would have been a few years before Margaret Hamilton reprised her Wicked Witch for an episode of *Sesame Street* only to have it pulled after the parents of terrified children complained. Such sissies wouldn't have lasted a week on Larcomb Drive, where the girls were boys and the boys were heroes or chain-smokers.

Today Mom looks like Cora, the longtime spokeswoman for Maxwell House Coffee, who was also played by—yes, you guessed it—Margaret Hamilton. I've never known Mom to be a coffee drinker, possibly because of Mamaw's far-fetched belief that—as babies who eat too many carrots and sweet potatoes can take on an orange hue—too much coffee could turn the drinker black.

* *

It was during Mom's first stay in the hospital where she coded the first two times that I quickly wrote the following magazine column, titled "Hey, Mom, I'm sorry." She loved it.

Hey, Mom, I know I shouldn't have given you that cave woman statuette with the word "MOM" inscribed on it for Mother's Day, no matter how funny I thought it was at the time. For that, I'm truly sorry.

I'm also truly sorry for "showing myself" in front of your friends—Oneida, Elizabeth, Ernestine, Marie, Sonja, Kitty, Margaret, the ladies from church, your PTA pals, Aunt Mabel, door-to-door sales people, Aunt Naomi. "Boy, you really showed yourself that time." I'm sorry for mocking you when you tried to set me straight.

I'm sorry for not telling you I love you as often as your granddaughter, Sydney, tells me she loves me, which is generally three or four times a day.

How many times did you repeat your curse upon me? "I only hope your kids are half as bad as you are." Guess what, Mom? You got that one right.

When I think about how bad I was and compare it to my own children, even when at their absolute, terrifying worst, it is about half as bad. If your curse is responsible for that blessing, thank you.

Again, I'm sorry.

I'm sorry for embarrassing you in front of your mother, who must have issued some curse on you other than the one you wished on me.

I'm sorry for leaving the personalized burgundy-and-gold letterman's jacket that you saved so much money for on the Greyhound bus trip to Tennessee, a trip that you paid for.

I'm sorry for signing up for that newspaper route that you and Dad had to help me with, and I'm sorry for adopting that dog the week before I left for college and leaving it for you and Dad to take care of.

I'm sorry for not picking up my dirty socks, and I'm sorry for seldom, if ever, saying thank you.

I'm so happy that I can tell you I'm sorry, and I only wish you hadn't had to wait so long to hear it.

Thank you for not getting any madder than you did when I made you repeatedly pull the Ford Fairlane over because I was hanging out of the passenger window like a cocker spaniel.

Thank you for simply rolling your eyes when I had store managers page you as lost over and over again in almost every store we ventured into. "ATTENTION WINN-DIXIE SHOPPERS. Little Stevie Vest is here at the front counter, again, and apparently his mother is lost . . . again."

Thank you for the soft-serve ice cream on the way home from the post office, thank you for the Dunkin' Donuts (chocolate honey-dipped) on our just-you-and-me road trip to Mississippi, and thank you for cutting my peanut butter and jelly sandwiches diagonally and wrapping them in wax paper. Thank you for the Oreo cookies.

I'm sorry for tracking mud into your house after you'd just scrubbed the kitchen floor.

I'm sorry for playing my music too loud and ignoring you when you asked me to turn it down.

I'm sorry for not telling you when I'd be late, and thank you for not slapping me across the face when I said, "Well, you raised me this way."

That was awful. A good slap might have done me good. Again, I'm sorry.

After all, you're the one who rushed me to the hospital when Jeff Worley shattered my collarbone; when that girl across the street cut off my fingertip by slamming her front door; and when my nose was crunched in seventh-grade gym and splattered so much blood you nearly fainted.

After all, you're the one who attempted to take on the neighborhood bullies and the mothers of the neighborhood bullies on my behalf. Again, I should have thanked you.

Mom, you were the one who listened to my silly dreams of becoming a professional baseball player (the next Johnny Bench), professional bowler (the next Earl Anthony), disc jockey (the next Coyote Calhoun), youth minister, international playboy, secret agent, best-selling author—all without laughing.

You were the one who picked me up after school even when you knew that I had intentionally missed the school bus. You were the one who took me to guitar lessons once a week for oh-so-many years even though I never learned how to play the guitar. You were the one who told me I shouldn't wear white socks with dress shoes. You were the one who pointed out when I was making a fool of myself over this silly girl or that silly girl and when I "better not let this one get away." "This one" is my loving wife of 22-plus years and the mother of my four "half-as-bad" children.

Thank you, Mom.

* *

During several of those deathbed moments, I could have eased Mom's pain by uttering five easy words. All I needed to do was say them and her suffering would be over. "You can *leeb* me now." I, however, couldn't bring myself to say it. I, like the Cowardly Lion, lacked the courage.

* *

Saying "well, you raised me this way" made Mom madder than anything else I could have possibly said. Oh, how that got under her skin.

Question: What kind of son would say such a thing?

Answer: An honest one.

The truth does hurt. It's an awful thing.

If I learned anything (get out your highlighter, this is important), to be a good and decent, upright person, you should never, under any circumstances, unless under a federal court order, tell the truth, the whole truth, and nothing but the truth. The truth is an awful thing.

* *

"Don't you dare lie to me," I heard more than once growing up. I never have lied, which is a lie. But, honestly, I cannot recall ever hearing Mom or Dad tell a lie. Never. Not once. They seldom told the truth, but they never lied. Now Mamaw, she always told the truth, without fail. If you looked fat, she'd tell you were fat. If you had food hanging from your nose, she'd announce it so all the Kapok Tree could hear. "Good Lord, boy, I hope to hell that's green beans."

"Mother," Mom would say.

"It's the truth," Mamaw would retort.

* *

Now for a little honesty. I love Mom and all of her quirks. I was shortsighted when I resented inheriting some, alright, most of them. In all the ways she once embarrassed me, I do likewise with my own children and sometimes I even enjoy it. Yes, I once wrongly believed Mom molded me into a coward with a paper-thin backbone, and by the time high school rolled around, she longed to be rid of me. "How could I want to get rid of you? You're my sweet boy."

But honestly I did think it. She seemed disappointed in me when on senior skip day I didn't go out and get in trouble. Instead I came home and watched game shows and soap operas with her. "Why don't you call up some of those friends of yours and go do something?" she'd say.

"Mom . . . What friends?"

I wrongly believed that Mom, with my consent, had systematically eliminated the friends I'd chosen for myself.

"Don't you think he's a little too wild?"

"Don't you think he's kinda shifty."

"What do we know, again, about his parents?"

"Where is it they live again?"

I took these questions to be Mom's sign of disapproval, which they may have been, but they were really only questions. It was my formulation of the potential answers that eliminated many of my acquaintances from evolving into friends. Maybe there weren't that many people good enough for Mom's little Stevie, but he had no idea who he was or what he wanted to be. Few teenagers do. He skated through high school and was ill-prepared for college, the military or the workforce. "Maybe you could get a job at the bowling alley," Mom once said. He— don't you hate it when people refer to themselves in the third person?—was destined for failure (or shoe rental), and that was perfectly fine by Mom. "Don't get your expectations too high," Mom said. "I'd oh-so hate for you to be disappointed."

How could I have missed the sarcasm? Being one of the most sarcastic people I know, seriously, how could I have taken everything Mom said so literally?

I believed that Mom created in me the spirit of a quitter, but I was a willing accomplice. A major lesson I learned from Mom was to avoid pain at all costs. The best way to avoid disappointment, no matter how small, is not to attempt a thing in the first place. If you never write the best-seller, it can't be rejected by agents and publishers. If you don't ask out the girls you really like, they can't say no. When do ask a girl out, flip it around and say 'You wouldn't want to go out with me, right?' That way they have to say yes to say no and you can just laugh it off like it was all just a joke. "You certainly wouldn't want to look foolish now, would you?"

When I wanted to try out for football: "You might get hurt. Don't you remember what Jeff Worley did to you when you played Smear the Queer in our backyard on Larcomb Drive?" The fact that I was a scrawny second-grader and he was a one-hundred-and-eighty-pound twelve-year-old in full football gear never came into the discussion. "Yeah Mom, you're probably right."

When I wanted to ride the big rides at the amusement park: "Remember what happened at poor little Troy's birthday party?"

Troy was a fellow second grader at Monticello Elementary School who invited me to his seventh birthday party, a trip to a traveling midway in the parking lot of Throckmorton's

Hardware Store in Huber Heights. Three spins of the Tilt-A-Whirl and I spewed everything from corndogs to cotton candy all over poor, little Troy's new birthday outfit. Not a drop on myself, but Troy, he was covered. "You should just feel awful," Mom told me later. "You absolutely ruined that poor little boy's birthday party, and his clothes will probably have to be thrown away."

Troy's was not the first nor last birthday I would destroy. The first was in Fort Lauderdale, Florida, where we once spent three solid weeks in the summer of 1965. Dad had accumulated too much vacation time with the Army Corps of Engineers, and was ordered to use it or lose it. A little girl in our complex, I think her name was Cindy, invited me to her unit for ice cream and cake, and during the opening of presents, I barfed all over her brand-new white birthday dress. "You should just feel awful," Mom said. "That little girl's dress was ruined. I wouldn't be surprised if you weren't invited to any more birthday parties."

When the first time came for me to host a first birthday party, I was also seven. I was allowed to invite seven guests, which Mom said was the perfect number. Not only did it match my age, it allowed for my chocolate cake with chocolate icing to be cut into eight even pieces. "Just right," I can hear Mom say. "Just right. Why would you want it any other way?"

Mom purchased prizes, games and invitations two weeks in advance, and we addressed and mailed them. Between the invitations being sent and the grand Saturday afternoon party, I had plenty of time to practice—and master—each of the games. I could drop a clothespin, held to the end of my nose, into a glass milk bottle from three stories up, backwards.

I was a party-game professional surrounded by rank amateurs. When the time came for the party games, I won them all. Each of the store-bought prizes: mine. "You should feel awful," Mom said afterward. Now, it might have been nice if, after my third or fourth decisive victory, if Mom would have pulled me aside and given a little life lesson in diplomacy, but no, everyone went home dejected and empty-handed. And ticked off. But no one spoke up because, after all, Mom was a witch, and at seven, everyone knows you don't mess with witches or, by extension, the sons of witches.

* *

Mom was witch-like for sure, but she was a pretty witch. She looked a little like Gypsy Rose Lee, whom Dad, and the rest of the crew of the USS *Caperton*, got to see while he was serving in the South Pacific.

Mom has been called many things. Darkly exotic is my favorite. "I got hired for a job at a department store in Cincinnati, but they let me go a few days later . . . when they realized I wasn't Jewish," she said. From the research I've done on her family, she's for the most part German with some Scot-Irish thrown in. In the early 1990s, she came down with a serious gallstone attack, and the doctor diagnosed her with *thalassemia*, also known as Mediterranean anemia. "It's a dominant gene, and each of you boys," he said, looking at us sons, "with your dark complexions, need to be aware of this as you get older. Now you blondes," he said, looking at two of my three nieces, "don't need to be too concerned." To the other niece, a carbon copy of Mom: "Watch out."

Since I've traced much of Mom's family back prior to 1700

without a sign of a single Mediterranean, a friend of mine who is a history buff suggested Mom might be a descendant of the Melungeons, who, according to a fairly well-documented legend, are descendants of Turks who were shipwrecked four hundred years ago and found kinship with the Cherokees. "You know," he said, "Elvis Presley and Abraham Lincoln were probably Melungeons."

Other than her witch-like features, the first time I realized Mom might look a little different than the other ladies in the Ellen C. Semple Elementary School PTA, of which she was a two-term president, was on the ride home from another three-week Florida vacation, in 1968, in the heat of the Civil Rights Movement.

Martin Luther King Jr. had been gunned down only months before. James Earl Ray had been arrested only weeks before. We, Mom, Dad and I, had spent 21 days on the beach and at the pool, and we—Mom and I—were quite delightfully brown as we headed up Interstate 75 through King's home state of Georgia.

In Perry—north of Unadilla and south of Macon—there was, and is, a Howard Johnson's with an attached Ho-Jo's Restaurant. We, I was told, were Howard Johnson's people. Holiday Inns were for fancier people, and Ramadas were for the rich. But, more importantly, Howard Johnson's was on the right side of the highway, and we never stopped on the left side of the road. Our entire trips were planned this way. There were places you stopped on the way down. There were places you stopped on the way back. But you never, under any circumstances, crossed the highway.

The other reason we were Howard Johnson's people was

that the Ho-Jo, with its orange roof and its Simple-Simon-and-the-Pie-Man signs, featured twenty-eight flavors of ice cream (lost on someone who ate only the signature orange sherbet), and Ho-Jo's served peanut-butter-and-jelly sandwiches for Little Stevie. "May he have his diagonally cut and served on wax paper?" I can imagine Mom asking a flustered waitress.

But no, what I actually remember is this. Mom was wearing a brand-new yellow pants suit with a broad white belt, and Dad and I were in our matching Bermuda shorts with white knit shirts.

"Three for lunch," Dad said before being asked, catching the hostess off guard.

After a long pause, a waitress, who looked at us with what now I can only describe as an inquisitive look, ushered us past numerous empty booths with place settings and menus to an empty table behind the accordion partition in the dark, windowless room generally reserved for Rotary, Kiwanis and Lions Club meetings.

When the waitress brought us water with crushed ice, Dad asked for menus and said, "The boy here would like a children's menu and some crayons, please."

In a huff, our waitress disappeared again and returned with the paper placemats, crayons and silverware she had obviously taken from another table, which was already adorned with such. From our isolated vantage point, we could hear other patrons being greeted and seated, but none were brought into our reserved area in the segregated shadows.

"We must be special," Mom said.

"Well, Marge, we're like royalty," Dad said.

Every so often a man would enter the room. He'd take

one step past the beige-colored accordion divider. He'd take a quick glance at Dad, a longer look at me and then a good, long, head-to-toe review of Mom. He'd then leave, and a few minutes later, another man would poke his head in and do the same thing.

"I don't know," we heard of the men say to another. "I just can't be sure. He's not, but she certainly could be."

Could be what? Dad: "Marge, you know, I think they must have you confused with some famous movie star."

CHAPTER II

Cutting the Grass

THE CLAMOR CAN OFTEN BE overwhelming.

Why is the television turned all the way up when no one is watching it? Why is the radio blaring so loud it can be heard over the television? Why are there five televisions in a three-bedroom house? Who is on the phone? Who is at the door?

"The cat wants in!"

"The cat wants out!"

"Molly—telephone!"

"Katy—get the door, please!"

"Chris! Has anybody seen Christopher?"

"I thought y'all were going to pick up this stuff."

"PHONE—somebody, please, get the phone!"

"Molly!"

"The cat wants back in!"

* *

When overwhelmed by the din created by chattering children, a clamoring spouse and/or the delegations that come with each, my old pal Clint escapes to a lonely creek or the Licking River in his handsome, handmade wooden canoe—the making of which suited the same need as the trips themselves. Pastor Dan slips off to the noisy machines of his southern Indiana woodshop. Fryrear takes a long ride on his chrome-muffled Harley. Some spend afternoons golfing. Others spend weekends hunting.

As for me, I cut grass.

Nothing cleans my cluttered skull like the mellow roar of my self-propelled Briggs & Stratton Troy-Bilt Tuff Cut 220. With its 21-inch blade and 6.75 horsepower motor, I can manicure the magnificently flat lawn around my palatial estate in less than 45 minutes—the perfect amount of separation needed to make my heart grow fonder, so to speak.

Cutting grass, the skills for which Dad taught me well, is the lone household chore I can do with limited preparation and without constant spousal supervision.

As I'm checking the 10w30 oil and putting unleaded gasoline in the tank, I call to Sydney, the youngest of my four children, to gather the collection of toys that have escaped from the playroom since the last mowing.

Sometimes, when I'm in a particularly foul mood, maybe once a cutting season, I mow the lawn without calling for Syd. The crunching and spewing of molded plastic cowboys, Indians and the occasional Polly Pocket brings a sadistic smirk to my face. I, for an instant, feel like the god of the Old Testament must have felt when the doors of Noah's ark were sealed and the first drops of rain started to fall. "It isn't like I didn't warn them," I think as the first plastic hand, molded head or booted foot spews forth toward the neighbor's weed-strewn fence.

It's fair to say that I need to cut the grass far more often than its growth requires.

*　*

During these 45-minute psychological health sessions, I am able to think, meditate on what is going well and what isn't in my over-scheduled personal and professional existence. I'm able to escape, to distance myself without once losing sight of those I hold dear, even those who have driven me into the exile of the mulching mower.

"Has anyone seen my cat?"

"Where is Christopher?"

"Someone answer the phone."

As the blade hacks its way through the backyard debris, grass and magnolia leaves, my mind is replenished with a patchwork of more pleasant memories.

As I maneuver carefully around the two maple trees Christopher and I planted as seedlings received at an Arbor Day celebration when he was a fourth-grade Cub Scout, I think of us crafting his less-than-aerodynamic Pinewood Derby racecar. I think of each of the Cub Scout campouts, the days when it was still okay for my all-too-cool son to spend aimless days with his witless father; the star-filled nights on the lawn of Old Fort Harrod or by the mountain shores of Lake McKee.

Stories told by the camp fire; corny skits; charred marshmallows; our less-than-stellar performance in the rain-gutter regatta, a showdown of homemade sailboats powered by puffing Scouts in blue uniforms fringed in yellow.

As I swipe back and forth under the canopy of our fragrant magnolia, which I am under the delusional belief is one of the Commonwealth's largest, I am, in my mind, traveling with nattily dressed Christopher and Katy across rural and rugged southern Indiana when my faded maroon Pontiac Grand Am, purchased from one of Dad's Gideon brothers, breaks down en route to a much-anticipated Smothers Brothers show.

As Christopher, maybe 12, fidgets in his tie and unaccustomed plaid blazer, the grease-coated, toothless truck mechanic leans in and asks me, "Hey, that boy of yours there. Does he go to one of them-there prep schools?"

The thought of happy-go-lucky Christopher at a rigid prep school, even now, makes me smile. Prep and Christopher are two words that have never before or since been uttered in connection.

* *

As I kick Molly's pink-and-pearl soccer ball out of the lawn-mower's path, I'm attempting to coach the Under-10 Dragons to victory on the perfectly manicured fields of Zoysia grass in Bowling Green. In way over our heads, the Dragons are pummeled in three games by a combined score of thirty-four to two. The Dragons were outscored, outplayed and, without question, out-coached. The girls, however, enjoyed the trip to the mall's arcade and ample food court so much that the memories of the slaughter were short-lived. "It was fun," said Sara Louise, one of the players upon whom a half-dozen of the goals were scored. "You know, coach, I can't wait until we do it again."

* *

In one pass across the lawn, I'm playing golf with my deceased father. "Hey, Dad, you want to hear the one about Moses and Jesus sneaking down from heaven to play Augusta National?"

"Oh, I like that one. How does it go again?"

In another swipe, Dad and I are fishing or in the Catonsville garage working on my own less-than-stellar Pinewood Derby car. "That, son, is by far the darndest thing I've ever seen."

One moment it's 1969, and my Mom and I are eating fresh, warm Krispy Kreme Original Glazed doughnuts with chocolate frosting on a road trip to see Dad in Mississippi. Dad has gone to help in the reconstruction following Hurricane Camille, a Category 5 storm that killed 259 people and caused $9 billion in damages. As we drive to Gulfport, hit hard by Camille, Mom and I are reading signs with missing letters as if they were totally new words—a grocery store named "rogers," a gas station called "hell."

The next pass, it's 1977, and Mom's trying to teach me how to drive. "Maybe we should wait until Dad gets home," Mom says as I back over the curb again in a failed effort to parallel park. "Or maybe Mike will take you driving. I'm not sure I have the patience for this. Did Dad ever tell you how he and Uncle Charles failed the first time they took their driver's test?"

"Yes, Mom. They got back in the truck and drove back home."

In a moment, I'm back to the present day and Sydney, my backseat navigator, is making short work of a small Wendy's Frosty. She is the age I was when eating chocolate doughnuts on the long trip with Mom. Then is now; now is then, and no more than a moment apart. We're traveling south through central Kentucky along US 27, and Syd spies out the rear passenger window an eight- to ten-foot fiberglass cow of the 1950s roadside variety. "Now, Dad," Syd says. "That has to be biggest cow I've ever seen in my entire life."

An hour or so later, Syd spots a similarly constructed fiber-glass cowboy, at least 20 feet tall, adorning the roof of a tire store. Why a tire store? I don't know. "Hey," Syd yells. "Dad, do you think he might be looking for his cow?"

*   *

As I mow along the back of the garage, it's October, and I'm sleeping with the windows open, and the only noise is the occasional hypnotic snap-crackle of the neighbors' bug zapper. Next, it's another distant Halloween, and Christopher is dressed as Pikachu, the most popular of all Pokemon, for the third consecutive year. The red, golden and brown leaves crunch under our feet as we shuffle across our neighbors' yards. "Hey, Dad, I was wondering. Is this one of those moments we'll always remember?"

"Yeah, buddy. I think so. I hope so."

*   *

Back at the estate, I'm finished with the grass. I brush off the lawnmower and return it to its reserved spot in the back of the cluttered garage. I am ready to rejoin the chaos that I'm certain awaits me through the metal storm door.

There will be battles over which cartoons to watch. "Hey, I was watching that!"

Or whose turn it is on the family room computer. "I was working on that. You had better have saved it."

"Has anyone seen my favorite hairbrush?" Katy screams from her second-floor bedroom.

"Why do you always think I took it?" counters Molly

from the basement. "Keep track of your own things and stop blaming other people for everything!"

"You're fat!"

"You're ugly!"

"Touch my stuff again and I'll kill ya," screams the elder.

"Good luck catching me," shouts the younger.

"Nobody's killing anybody. You two stop right now."

"Telephone. Would someone please answer the phone!"

There's the sound of a slamming door. There is the rumble of loud footsteps on the stairs. "MOM!"

The good news is that there is always more grass to be cut. Maybe, however, just in case, I should learn how to use the leaf blower.

CHAPTER 12

Mom for the Defense

No MATTER WHERE I SAT on the crowded Catonsville, Maryland, mustard-yellow school bus, the older of the two Buckley brothers would find a way to sit directly behind me. At every opportunity, my nemeses would flick hard the tender tops of my slightly pointed, protruding ears, again and again and again. With each unprovoked flick he would scream in his nasally high-pitched voice "Prick!"

Sometimes, like in the Westchester Elementary School hallway, he would sneak up behind me and shout "Prick!" if no teachers were around or whisper it if they were, without the flick, and I would flinch all the same.

When I went home crying and asked the meaning of the repeated insult, it was Mom who explained prick was a less-than-polite word for what Mom called my "privates."

Dad said I should pray for both of the Buckley brothers, because it was obvious from the way they acted they were unhappy with themselves. For years, I did pray for the older one, for him to get what was coming to him.

When I told Mom I couldn't get Bigger Buckley to stop and asked her what I should do, she went to Montgomery Ward and bought me a navy blue Baltimore Colts Super Bowl V championship sock cap.

* *

To be fair, Mom did the best she could with the tools available. Self-esteem is not something someone else can give you. I've learned that. It can be fostered. It can be bruised. But it is what it is. When it is virtually stripped from someone, as it was with Mom by Mamaw, it's difficult, near impossible, to overcome. How can you bolster someone else's self-esteem when you have none of your own?

With Mom, there were always ten reasons to one in choosing not to do something. I never did most—well, any—of the things most teenagers do until years after it was fashionable—or normal—to do them. I never thought much about—I never much read—anything, really, that might challenge my limited, sheltered perspective.

* *

When the time came for me to compete, I never tried too hard. I didn't want to make anyone else feel bad. When you can't figure out how to be a gracious winner, it's much easier and self-deprecating to be a gracious loser. As a Webelos Scout, I was once presented eleven activity badges at one meeting. I was embarrassed. I had the same feeling when I was elected to the Order of the Arrow, Boy Scouts' highest honor; president of my college fraternity, the Interfraternity Council, and my high school's hall of fame. The same feeling accompanied each and every writing or journalism award I've earned. When it came time to be excited or thrilled, I would shy away, not because I wasn't pleased, but because, maybe deep down inside, I just didn't want to throw up on anyone. When I asked my wife to marry me, I never actually asked her. I shielded myself from probable rejection by asking her when and where "someone" should get married. I approached her as if I was doing research, and she somehow, patiently, lovingly, put the pieces together.

"Look," she said. "If someone were to get married on the 22nd of November, a Saturday, they'd only have to take three days vacation before the Thanksgiving Day weekend. Yes, June is the traditional time when most people get married, but as you can see, November is just perfect. Who would want it any other way?"

* *

When I was in the eighth grade, Mom got a job in the school cafeteria, as she had at three of my six elementary schools. She said it was to give her something to do—to get out of the house—but I'm not buying it now any more than I bought it then. She was there to make sure I didn't get hurt. Her fear of something bad happening has made her miss out on so many things.

* *

Mom was born March 1, 1927 in Covington, Kentucky, and named after a "pretty baby" Mamaw saw in the quarterly L&N Railroad magazine. From birth until the summer day in 1945 she married my father, she lived at home. She lived with some combination of Dad or Dad and us three boys until Dad's death in 2002. It was then that Mom lived alone for the first time. It was then, for the first time, she knew how scared she was. Until then, she could be afraid for us, our children and our children's children. Now, her greatest fear is that something will happen to her—something embarrassing and humiliating—and, being alone, we won't know right away. Since the ill-advised trip to the hospital, she's also afraid to get too far away from a restroom.

Mom has always, like Mac before her, lived with the fear of something unknown, so awful it cannot be expressed. Yes, she's hiding something. She begins to tell you a story, and once you're entranced, it ends without reaching any conclusion. You're left to fill in the pieces, some of which can be substantial.

During Mom's most recent hospital stay, we were talking about colleges and if she'd ever had any interest in attending one. "I visited one once," she said. "I went with Joyce over to the University of Cincinnati, and I don't know where we were—maybe it was a fraternity house . . . it certainly was a party."

Her tone indicates that she wasn't too impressed with what she saw and was certain she wouldn't have missed out on anything by not going.

"You know," she said later, "Joyce went to college in New Orleans—what is it, Tulane? I was working at General Electric in Cincinnati. That was while your father was still away in the Navy, and Mother let me go visit Joyce. I was surprised she'd let me go, but I rode all the way to New Orleans on the train. I was walking along Canal Street. Joyce was in class, and I saw this boy we met at the party in Cincinnati [840 miles northeast] coming the other way."

"Well, that's certainly a coincidence," I said. "What did you say?"

"Oh, I didn't say anything. I turned and went the other direction as quickly as I could."

"Are you sure it was him? It could have been someone who looked like him."

"Oh, no, I was sure."

The point of this story is unclear to me, but I can't help but be reminded of her fear of snakes. She often tells about a time she walked from one grandmother's house in the foothills of northern Kentucky to the other, a distance of more than four miles, four hilly miles, only to turn back because she saw, at a distance, a black snake in the road.

"Are you sure it wasn't a stick?"

"Oh no, I was sure."

*   *

While I never once heard Dad cuss, Mom occasionally let an "oh, hell" slip by, and twice in my memory, she said "damn." The second time, I was a freshman in high school, and she came upon me feeling up a neighbor girl in the space between our brick house and Dad's 1973 Cutlass Supreme Oldsmobile. "Boy," she said as I turned 57 varieties of red, "you're making a fool of yourself in front of the whole damned neighborhood."

The first time came a year or so earlier, the second summer after we returned to Kentucky. The Crabbmyers, a large, all-boy, Catholic family across the cul-de-sac, adopted me as a project, much the way Bigger Buckley had in Catonsville.

Whenever Mom and Dad and I returned from church or Scouts or after-school activities, one of the Crabbmyers, hidden from view, would yell "Stevie, oh Stee-v-ie" and cackle. They would call late at night and hang up. They would hoot and whistle anytime Mom was out in our yard.

That particular summer day, I was playing football with

Benny and a dozen of the other neighborhood kids, including Fryrear and Dorsey and the girl I felt up a year later, in my parents' driveway. The youngest of the Crabbmyers asked to join in. When he was knocked to the ground, minutes later, he ran home claiming I'd taken a cheap shot, which maybe I had. He was a head shorter than I was, making him an easy target.

Younger Crabbmyer returned with his brother, a head taller than me, to exact his revenge.

I blocked punch after punch. Football was one thing. Fighting was another. I knew Dad would be disappointed if he learned I'd been fighting, so I was content to just defend myself. Bigger Crabbmyer threw rights, which I ducked. His much weaker lefts, I blocked with my forearms. I fended off blow after blow. Mom appeared in our front storm door and Momma Crabbmyer appeared in the glass door across the street.

Bigger Crabbmyer, still rather robotic, increased the frequency and ferocity of his attack, while Smaller Crabbmyer urged him on. Benny and the gang swirled around us, anticipating a blood-letting. Crabbmyer landed a glancing jab here and there. My forearms began to sting as I continued my defensive rope-a-dope posture. "He's got to be getting tired," I thought, assuming he'd just go home when he got bored with my unwillingness to fight back. I knew deep down that he was simply following orders. Sure, I didn't like him, but he was probably justified, at least this time, in standing up for his little brother.

Sweat ran down his pock-marked forehead, and with each muted punch, he grunted louder and louder. Under his foul breath, he muttered either *prick* or *dick*.

Mom, her face pinched in anger, stepped onto the front porch and shocked me when she shouted, "Damn it, Stevie, hit him back."

I half-expected her to tell me to stop, being like my father, but she didn't. I, however, could see it in her deep, dark brown eyes.

"Stee-v-ie," Bigger Crabbmyer mockingly repeated. "Stee-v-ie."

I took a half-step backwards and swung my clenched bony fist with years of repressed anger, landing my first, and only, right cross squarely on Bigger Crabbmyers's pock-marked left cheek with a force that caused his recently installed braces to explode, or unhinge, inside his clutched jaw.

His black, lifeless, raven-like eyes grew wide. He stepped back, paused. He slowly raised his hands to his puckered mouth, turned on the heels of his black Chuck Taylors and ran for home, sobbing. I was certain he had lost several teeth to my rage. I felt sick to my stomach.

Mom shuffled down our driveway in the direction of the Crabbmyers' house. Momma Crabbmyer came out on her porch and warned Mom not to come any further.

"Control that idiot kid of yours," Momma Crabbmyer bellowed.

"And you, you control yours," Mom responded.

Momma Crabbmyer barked something about us getting an orthodontist bill, which we never did, but I believe that was the last day anyone in our house, or out, called me Stevie.

* *

Of the many things of which I'm ashamed, the fact that when I was younger I found Mom an embarrassment is one. I know many who say it's a parent's job to embarrass their children. She did her job well—still does. She makes a lot of noise and draws a lot of attention. She's adorned with dozens of rings and plastic bracelets and the way she smacks her Dentyne Cinnamon Chewing Gum again and again.

I guess that's why, in middle school, I intentionally missed the bus home so often—almost every day. Yes, I had an emerging interest in a long-haired brunette named Wendy, the same one as from my first car date several years later, whom I walked home from school, but it also afforded me an hour— maybe ninety minutes—alone, before Mom came looking for me. "I was afraid something might have happened to you," she would say day after day after day.

*   *

I learned valuable lessons from a cadre of people—Mamaw, Mac, Dad, Mike, Tim, teachers, preachers, Mom's friends, parents and kids at church, classmates at school—but Mom was the filter through which each of their lessons was sifted. Mamaw, Dad, and Mom were like the legs of a three-legged stool. If any leg is stronger or weaker than another, you have no balance whatsoever. You might be able to rest on it for a while, but you better not stand on it or you'll certainly bust your ass.

Despite Mamaw's belief that the world was black and white, cut and dried, nothing could be further from the truth. Most of the lessons I learned from Mamaw could be classified as bad or negative, and most of the lessons I learned from Dad were good or positive. Both lessons were filtered through Mom, who unfortunately has no filter of her own. Like Mac's cigarettes, her logic and enlightenment were rolled by hand.

*   *

Mom and I agreed to disagree on the showdown between Mamaw and Aunt Mabel. She has her story. I have mine. Sure, I thought I had the clear memory, but if, as Mom claimed, the sisters' relationship collapsed in a dispute over a ceramic Santa sleigh and reindeer, who was I to question it? The issue was put to rest, so to speak.

During our most recent Christmas visit to the condominium Mom calls home, she asked me—of all people—if I'd be interested in Mamaw's Christmas card collection. "I've got to clear out some of this stuff," she said.

"I'm not sure what I'd do with them, Mom," I said of the cards, some dating back 50 years, as I took the seat I generally occupy during my frequent visits, one with an unobstructed view of Mom's blaring 42-inch Sanyo television. That wasn't really true. Not knowing what I would do with the Christmas cards is family code for I'd probably—most likely—throw them away. I certainly have enough of my own junk, and I, too, need to get rid of some stuff.

From my perch, I am able to focus on the television and remain oblivious to most of the ongoing conversations and generally ignorant of my surroundings. I sometimes like it that way, disconnected. We'd been at Mom's for more than an hour when Kay said to Mom, "You know, I've never seen this before. Can you tell me about it?"

"Oh, yes," Mom said, with a certain giddiness in her voice I had almost forgotten she possessed. "Well, you know, my

Aunt Mabel had quite a way with ceramics, and she made one of those for each of her sisters. That's the one she made for Mamaw. Isn't it beautiful?"

Breaking the television's hypnotic hold, I was amazed to see, for the first time, less than three feet away, the quite legendary Santa in White Ceramic Sleigh, With Reindeer, more than four feet long with nine, not eight, reindeer, each individually more than four inches long, attached with dark red reins, black bridles, and brass rings and bits.

There's Dasher and Dancer.

There's Prancer and Vixen.

Comet and Cupid. Donder and Blitzen.

And yes, if you may recall, there's the most famous reindeer of all, too, pulling a jolly ceramic Saint Nicholas in a wooden sleigh stacked high with presents for good boys and girls. Each reindeer has his head cocked slightly left. I assume the pose is so each of the reindeer is facing the viewer, but Mom has them situated so they're looking out the window, enjoying the view of the gardens below and the not-so-distant Ponder Creek that separates her adult living community from the nearby nursing home.

From my close inspection, I can see that, somewhere in the past 40-plus years, Vixen's antlers have had an incident that has required them to be reattached with glue, but other than that, each of Aunt Mabel's creations glistens as if fresh out of the kiln.

It was: Exhibit No. 1 in "The Case of the Porcelain Present." I was Perry Mason for the defense, and Mom, a most unreliable witness, had finally slipped up. If the sleigh had, in fact, been given to an insignificant neighbor in Florida, as Mom boldly claimed, how did it end up in Mom's apartment in Kentucky? Had it always been here? Had I simply overlooked it, like so many things, for more than 40 years?

"Mom," I said, flustered and amazed, with a certain gotcha tone in my voice.

What to do? I had Mom right where I wanted her. Somewhere in my enhanced memory of the moment is the slowly rising cadence of kettledrum. The camera pans the crowded courtroom, which is a strange mixture of Mason's cadre of California courtrooms, the one from *Miracle on 34th Street*, and the one strolled by Atticus Finch in Maycomb County, Alabama, in *To Kill A Mockingbird*. Among those in attendance are Aunts Naomi and Mabel, wearing matching blouses from Macy's, standing just inside the courtroom door. Mac, rolling a cigarette, is to their right, keeping an eye on young Mike and Tim, tugging at their stiff collars. The camera zooms in on Dad, wearing his white Navy uniform. He is seated three rows behind the defendant's table, attentive, but silent. Mamaw is just over the prosecutor's right shoulder next to Agnes Moorehead. Audrey and Agnes, smirking, are wearing large, matching hats with netting, obstructing the view of those behind them. After a quick pan of the balcony full of black nursing home employees, black and white waiters and waitresses and storeclerks, Jem and Scout Finch, young Natalie Wood, Neighbor in his tattered T-shirt, and cousins, it flashes to Mom in her burgundy recliner, which is oddly out of place behind the defendant's table in a darkly paneled courtroom. Is that Gregory Peck?

Mom, unaware of her misstep—the precarious position— the obvious conclusion that "her goose is cooked," is smacking her Dentyne gum and fiddling with her multi-colored bracelets.

The courtroom version of me fidgets in uncomfortable black dress shoes and itchy dress pants, picked out by Mamaw for such an important occasion. I hem and haw and wring my hands beneath a portrait, not of George Washington or Abraham Lincoln, but of the kindly white-haired doctor painted again and again by Norman Rockwell.

Had Mom pulled a Valdosta-style lie on me? Had she issued two independent facts to hide a greater truth? Had she maybe said something like, "You know Aunt Mabel made some sets for her neighbors" coupled with "When Mamaw said she didn't want hers, she gave it to someone else"? So, was Mom that someone? Could it be that that truth would expose a forbidden visit to Aunt Mabel?

I knew what Perry Mason would do. I certainly knew what Mamaw would do.

Then, after a moment of consideration, I wondered—I couldn't help it—if Dad were really here, what would he do?

I brought my thin, fidgety fingers to my chin as if I were pondering something profound to say, and then I turned to my right and said, "You know, Mom, that really is beautiful."

CHAPTER 13

Car Trouble

STANDING AT THE END OF an informal receiving line to the right of my father's casket, Brockman—a friend since junior high school—said, "You know, Steve, today you are a man."

"What?" I thought. "I'm 40 years old with four children of my own, and *today* I am a man? What kind of friend would say such a thing?"

The answer: (again) an honest one.

When Dad left home in the spring of 1940, he never asked anyone—especially his family—for anything. That's something Dad shares in common with my son Christopher, who left home last summer, opting for a full-time processing job over his parents' dream of him going to college, at least for now. "I want to be on my own," Christopher said. "I don't know for sure what I want to do, but I want to follow my own dreams, and I don't expect you and Mom to help."

That was never the case with me. Mom once said that I was born with my hand out. What Brockman knew, I suspect, is that, while I was out on my own, raising my family and holding down a cadre of jobs—certainly looking the part of a buttoned-down grownup—I could, and knew I could, at any time call on Dad for help. As long as Dad was around, I had a safety net, which, according to the Flying Wallendas' Nik Wallenda, is not always a good thing because of the false security it offers. With Dad gone, I'd have to stand on my own two feet without any sense of security, false or otherwise. Now I would have to be my own man.

When Christopher moved out in July before his 19th birthday, I secretly—like most fathers, I suspect—longed for him to call asking for my help. Not so I could say "I told you so," because I had never told him there was anything he couldn't do, and there was nothing, at least legal, I felt he shouldn't try. Christopher was, I hope and pray, raised with a gumption and determination I never had. If it was his dream to be a rock-star guitarist with a dozen tattoos and a gauge in his ear, despite what others may think, that's what he should be. But still, I wanted Christopher to admit on some level that he needed me. I wanted to know that, as a father, I had some value. I wanted to know that, as a man, I had some worth.

Sure, I attempted to raise Christopher to be self-sufficient, but no father really wants that. Maybe a mother bird can raise her hatchling without emotion and boot its sorry ass from the nest, never to be seen again, but not any red-blooded American dad. We—I assume, since I haven't spoken to all other fathers, yet—revel as much in our sons' shortcomings and failures as we do in their achievements and successes. It allows us to see ourselves as the younger misfits we once were and for at least an instant pretend that we've put those days of uncertainty, immaturity, and misfortune behind us; that we have, in some sense, become our fathers, whether that is a good, bad, or indifferent thing.

When Christopher called in November to ask for a "big, big favor," I took a deep breath. I braced myself for something monumental, life-threatening: an embarrassing infestation needing immediate medical treatment, an unplanned pregnancy, an impending lawsuit, bail. Something major, right?

It turned out that Christopher had left his headlights on all day while working part-time in the Kroger deli, and he needed a jumpstart with my jumper cables. When I sent him forth into the world prepared with the tools he would need, jumper cables and a carjack were not on the list. He needed me. A case could be made that he didn't need me but my jumper cables, but that would be a defeatist attitude on my part, so I hold onto the self-centered delusion a little bit longer.

"No problem, buddy," I said. "I'll be there as quickly as I can."

Filled with a sense of exhilaration that my son did, for once, need me, I finished my work, and within minutes I was out the door and en route across town to the Kroger parking lot, where I found my son being helped by two of his coworkers who had moments before happened along. "Hey, Dad," Christopher shouted upon seeing me. "These guys had some cables, so I'm covered. Thanks anyway."

His car was a rather used little faded red rag-top, which let in just as much sun and rain with the top up or down. But he had bought the convertible with his own money, so I had no real say in the matter. Now, it was already started. He climbed in, waved, and sped away, leaving me to contemplate my place in the world from the vantage point of a crowded grocery store parking lot. It was apparent that even the speed in which I delivered assistance was not meeting the standards Dad had set.

My fatherhood bar was set rather high, and it was going to take much more effort on my part to ever reach it. It was unfair, really. I can't even remember asking Dad for help. I mean, really, there weren't cell phones back then, so I'm not even sure how he knew I needed him. He would just appear, offer his silent assistance, and disappear. Not all, but most of my problems involved used cars.

My first car mishap happened on a Saturday night, two blocks from my parents' house. I was driving home from a date when I rear-ended a carload of hooligans who, like me, were gazing upon the wonder that was long-legged blonde Debbie McMillin, a twenty-something vision of tanned lust in a sprayed-on costume.

There she was, glorious, in a pair of white shorty-shorts, descending the embankment outside of Champ's Roller-drome, the place itself the subject of a cornucopia of adolescent sexcapades, or at least, the fantasies of such. My glimpse of big-haired Debbie, a Roller Derby version of Suzanne Somers (vintage 1978) came out of the corner of my left eye, just before I slammed into the car in front of me, a rusted-out Dodge, which had come to a complete stop without any hint of brake lights.

Debbie was spectacular. She had long, golden locks and inch-long eyelashes accenting her big blue eyes. My father's generation would have called her a bombshell. In 1978: a brick house. She was mighty-mighty, letting it all hang out. Dirty old men, and those who someday aspired to be such, traveled from distant parts of the county to watch her prance around the softball bases in her strained mesh jersey and similarly strained skin-tight white shorts. For her to appear in my window was as close as I'd get to having Farrah Fawcett—other than the poster above my bed—waiting for me at home.

The scruffy guys in the other car claimed they hadn't even seen her. They told the police officer that I had just crashed into them for no reason whatsoever. They were apparently just minding their own business, parked in the middle of a well-traveled suburban highway. While I was clearly at fault given that I rear-ended them, there was a reason, although, to my parents' insurance company, not a very good one. "Well, you see, there's this girl named Debbie McMillin," I imagine my father beginning to explain over the kitchen wallphone. "Debbie McMillin!" interrupts the insurance adjuster. "Debbie McMillin, the softball player? She's spectacular. Oh, what I wouldn't give to get with that. Have you seen her throw? When she goes to scoop up a ground ball . . . damn, man, you haven't seen her?"

How I called Dad to break the news that I had wrecked his newly acquired 1973 Cutlass Supreme Oldsmobile is a mystery to me. As I've noted, there were no cell phones then, and Eddie's Seafood House, where the Oldsmobile came to rest, was long closed at that hour.

As I think back on it, I'm not even sure how Dad got to Eddie's Seafood House. Maybe he walked, or maybe we still had the Country Squire station wagon, and maybe I just refused to drive it anymore, not wanting my date to see me for what I was, someone who drove not-so-lightly-used cars.

But Dad was there, and he helped me talk to the police, exchange insurance information, and get the Cutlass Supreme home so it could be hauled away later for massive repair. It was a mess. The hood was peeled back and the front bumper was bent downward in a pouty smile, leaving the radiator exposed like a big, toothy, mocking grin.

I was hard on cars, especially Dad's. I was none too kind to the Country Squire, the Cutlass Supreme, or the Dodge Coronet. When Dad was willed a white recreational vehicle while I was in college, I drove it to football tailgate parties at the fairgrounds. We put kegs in the small shower, and I allowed my fraternity brothers to party on the roof until it leaked. When Dad asked if anyone had been on the roof, I responded honestly: "I never saw a single person on the roof." A dozen people, maybe more, but a single one, no, never. You know, the Buckleys were right: I really was a prick.

Once, while I was in college, one of my coworkers, Shelonda, a six-foot-two, 125-pound woman of obvious African descent, had an important errand to run, and I, against my upbringing, allowed her to borrow the white 1969 Buick Skylark that had long been Mamaw's prized possession.

Mamaw had hoped to trade it in on a new car, but with all of the time it had spent in the humidity of Florida, it was rusted beyond worthless despite having fewer than 15,000 miles on the odometer.

"You know, Mother, Steve could use a car," Mom said when the salesman said he wouldn't give her more than a few dimes and pennies for it in trade.

"Well then," Mamaw said. "Stevie certainly won't be able to say I never gave him anything."

The sight of Shelonda behind the wheel of Mamaw's big satin-white car made me smirk and laugh to myself. I could just hear Mamaw's reaction. "How could you let that old black thing drive my sweet Lady Bird?"

When Shelonda returned the Skylark, she parked it going the wrong way—why, I do not know—across the street from the copy store where we worked. As she got out of the Skylark with a large stack of papers and a bag of McDonald's fare, she accidentally dropped my keys into a grated storm drain. Again, I can't even remember calling Dad. Somehow, however, Dad was there, equipped with a large magnet and a long piece of twine, and after several tries, he successfully fished my keys out of the dark, murky water. No sooner than I could turn around, Dad was gone.

I'm certain I didn't have time to say "thank you" then, but I'm not sure if I ever even thanked him for anything. Probably not. In one of the parables contained in the 13th chapter of Matthew, Jesus says that, contrary to popular belief, you don't always reap what you sow. That was the case with Dad, I guess. While Dad and I certainly made our peace if any needed to be made, ultimately he deserved better than he got.

While he sowed quality seed only to see his field peppered with weeds, Mom's garden was bountiful with what she expected, the worst.

She loves to tell about the day when I went on a quest to have a new cassette player and sound system put into Mamaw's Skylark. She says that I asked, pleaded, for her to follow me to a remote stereo installation center on the opposite side of town. I needed her, she said, on the off chance that they might need to keep the car and I might find myself in need of being somewhere else.

We lost each other in rush-hour traffic, and by the time she caught up with me twenty minutes or several hours later, depending on to whom she's telling the story, I seemed perplexed, even embarrassed, to see her. "What on Earth are *you* doing here?" I reportedly asked in a huff, and rather indignantly—at least in her spot-on, snarky impersonation of me. "Can't you see that Kay [my new girlfriend at the time] is here, and she can give me a ride if I need one? Good Lord, Mom, I'm 23 years old. I think I can take care of myself!"

CHAPTER 14

The Final, Lonely Whistle

MAMAW'S LAST LIVING SIBLING, AUNT Naomi, died in the winter of 2011. At Aunt Naomi's funeral is a five-year-old boy with a big, goofy grin and a short, spiky haircut. He is occupied with a blue Hot Wheels car and seemingly oblivious to the significance of the day's events.

During the post-graveside lunch at a northern Kentucky restaurant called the Greyhound Tavern, which has become a family tradition having hosting similar luncheons following the graveside services for Dad and Mamaw, his toy car gets away from him and rolls in my direction. "It's mine now," I jokingly announce. He sees right through me. He snatches his car and chuckles.

Throughout lunch we exchange funny faces. I beg for "my" car back. He taunts me with it but refuses to let it leave his grasp. I know from my great-aunt's (his great-grandmother's) obituary that his name is Nathan.

An hour earlier, the funeral home in Cheviot, Ohio, was filled with photo collages of Aunt Naomi and Uncle Skeeter; their son, Tom; their twin granddaughters, and their two great-grandchildren. My attention was focused on a picture of Uncle Skeeter, who had passed away six or seven years earlier, when the pastor quoted John 14:26, which mentions "remembrance" and asked that we, the gathered grievers, continue to tell the stories of the times we've shared with those who have died. "As long as we do that, they're still with us," he said, justifying, in some small way, my chosen vocation.

You see, Uncle Skeeter, who worked for a greeting card company, was one of the few extended relations to openly encourage my practice of writing about family. "These people," he often said, rolling his eyes, "are . . . well, certainly worth writing about. Bless their pea-picking hearts."

Naomi, my grandmother's youngest sister, was, in stark contrast to my grandmother, an extremely positive person. In contrast to her husband, she was tall and regal. Uncle Skeeter was a little fella like me who made funny faces.

Skeeter's given name was Edgar, but somewhere along the line someone said he was "no bigger than a skeeter" (as in mosquito). Imagine, if you can, Morey Amsterdam, Buddy Sorrell on *The Dick Van Dyke Show*, married to Doris Day.

At Aunt Naomi's graveside service, maybe 30 yards from Dad, Mac and Mamaw's markers, the pastor repeated a story Tom had told him about attending my grandfather Mac's funeral in 1967. Mac was an engineer for the Louisville & Nashville Railroad. As the pastor closed his prayer and Mac was being lowered into the ground, a long, soulful train whistle sounded through the trees to the west of the Forest Lawn Memorial Park in Erlanger. Someone commented that it was Mac's way of saying goodbye and reminding us he was still with us.

I don't remember that.

I was then Stevie, a five-year-old boy playing with an assortment of Matchbox cars, a Mercedes Truck, a Safari Land Rover, a Ford Mustang Fastback, a Formula 1 Lotus, a white

Mercedes 230SL and a Ferrari Berlinetta. Man, I loved my Matchbox cars—well, at least until Hot Wheels arrived on the scene.

I do remember train's whistle sounding during Mamaw's funeral in 2006, and someone—I think it was my witty sister-in-law, Mike's wife—saying it was Mac returning to escort dear, sweet Mamaw home. I could imagine "or to run her over" running through the mind of an immature person with a cadre of unresolved childhood issues, but luckily, no such persons were among the mourners.

We, the extended family, see each other only at funerals. That's the way it is with many families nowadays. We talk about getting together, but the weeks turn into months and the months into years, and the once tight-knit family continues to unravel. We're not strangers, but we're certainly not a part of each other's daily lives.

Aunt Naomi's twin granddaughters, Linda and Lisa—my second cousins—have never been in any of the dozen houses I've lived in over the years. I've never been in any of theirs. Our connections are rooted in the Great Depression and World War II, years before any of us were born. Which one of them is Nathan's mother would be a wild guess on my part.

Our time between visits is often a decade or more. The preschooler of one visit is the high school graduate of the next. As one generation passes, the lore, the traditions, fade.

They know nothing of my deep-sea fishing trip with Uncle Skeeter and how he said I threw up better than anyone else he'd ever seen. "Boy, that was really something," he said on our return to the Clearwater Marina. Mussing my hair, as he always did, he snickered, "Damn, boy, I think you actually scared the fish."

The sisters know little of the sibling rivalry between my grandmother and theirs. The vast age differences within the generations have left us oddly aligned. Tom sees my mom as an aunt instead of as a cousin. I'm closer in age to his daughters, but old enough, to them, to be just some old guy they see only at funerals and weddings. But I don't recall attending their weddings, and I'm pretty sure they didn't attend mine.

Back home in Frankfort, where I have lived for more than a decade, I try to gather my thoughts on the meaning of the day's events. I am drawn back to Nathan and the silly faces we shared. To him, I am a nameless, funny old man with double-jointed fingers. I am now Uncle Skeeter. Nathan is now me.

In the distance, a long, soulful train whistle echoes through the limestone of the Kentucky River Valley, and it is time for bed.

Acknowledgements

This book owes a great deal to Ted Sloan, Lynn Pruett and Journey McAndrews for their guidance, patience and encouragement; Christine Hale, for showing me how to break stories apart and put them back together again; and Karen McElmurray, for urging me to venture into corners I initially did not think I wanted to go. Much is also owed to poet Nickole Brown and writers Dinty W. Moore, Squire Babcock and Tommy Hays.

To all those who put up with me during the process—my family (especially those portrayed in the book), my loving Mom (without whom this book would not be possible), my wife Kay, my brothers, neighbors, and cousins.

To my current and former coworkers at *Kentucky Monthly*, especially Kendall Shelton, Kim Butterweck, Amanda Hervey, Lindsey McKinney, Patricia Ranft, and Michael Embry.

My fellow MFA students at Murray State University, especially James B. Goode, Carrie Gaffney, Cintia Sutton, Jacklyn Dre Marceau, Melissa Blankenship, Tim Stair, and Lisa Jones Luton.

And thanks to those who read and offered constructive suggestions, including, but not limited to, Carol Butler, designer Eric Butler, Alan Krome, Katy Vest, Dr. Gene Burch, Ronda Sloan, Laura Begin, Sheryl Vanderstel, Susan Siegel, Debbie

Acknowledgements

Jeffries Reece, Vince Staten (who once told me that having a long list of acknowledgements helps sell books), Ed McClanahan, Sena Jeter Naslund, Karen Lafer Haithcock, Tom Stephens, and Lessing J. Rosenwald, whoever and wherever you are.

Bibliography

Black, Carol, and Neal Marlens. *The Wonder Years*. Television.

Bombeck, Erma. *The Grass Is Always Greener over the Septic Tank*. New York: McGraw-Hill, 1976.

Bowers, Ronald L. "Agnes Moorehead Thinks Acting Is More A Matter of Magic than of Craft." *Tripod | Error*. May 17, 2011. <http://samstephens.tripod.com/agnes.html>.

Emerson, Ralph W. "Finish Each Day and Be Done with It."

"FASTSTATS—Birthweight." *Centers for Disease Control and Prevention*. May 19, 2011. <http://www.cdc.gov/nchs/fastats/birthweight.htm>.

"Find A Grave—Millions of Cemetery Records and Online Memorials." *Find A Grave—Millions of Cemetery Records*. May 17, 2011.

"Interview with Charles Tranberg—Bewitched @ Harpies Bizarre." *Bewitched @ Harpies Bizarre – www.harpiesbizarre.com*. May 17, 2011. <http://www.harpiesbizarre.com/tranberg_interview.htm>.

Johnson, E. Polk. *A History of Kentucky and Kentuckians*. Chicago: Lewis Pub., 1912.

Mancine, Ben. "The Kapok Tree Inn." *Ben's Place*. 2008. May 15, 2011. <http://benzplace.com/kapok/>.

Moore, Dinty W. *Between Panic and Desire*. Lincoln: University of Nebraska, 2008.

————. *Crafting the Personal Essay: a Guide for Writing and Publishing Creative Nonfiction*. Cincinnati, Ohio: Writer's Digest, 2010.

Olson, Robin. "The Truth behind the Poem 'Success,'" *Welcome to Robin's Web*. August 31, 2001. May 19, 2011. <http://www.robinsweb.com/truth_behind_success.html>.

"Perry Mason." *Wikipedia, the Free Encyclopedia*. May 15, 2011. <http://en.wikipedia.org/wiki/Perry_Mason>.

Pitts, William S. "The Church in the Wildwood," popularly known as "The Brown Church in the Vale." 1857.

Sherman, Richard M., and Robert B. Sherman. "It's A Small World." Disney. Recorded 1964.

Shields, David. *The Thing about Life Is That One Day You'll Be Dead*. New York: Vintage, 2009.

Tin Can Sailors—The National Association of Destroyer Veterans. May 17, 2011. <http://www.destroyers.org/smrdd/USS_Caperton.html>.

Urban, Keith. "Who Wouldn't Want to Be Me?" by Monty Powell. Recorded 2000. *Golden Road*. Capitol Records, 2002.

USS Caperton. Web. 17 May 2011. <http://www.usscaperton.info/>.

Vest, Harold G. "Testimonial." Wednesday evening prayer meeting. Parkwood Baptist Church, Louisville, Kentucky. July 2002.

Vest, Stephen M. "I'm Sorry Momma." *Kentucky Monthly* May 2009. Print.

————. "Mamaw Memories." *Kentucky Monthly* December 2007.

About the Author

Stephen M. Vest is the editor, publisher and founder of *Kentucky Monthly* magazine, which won the Governor's Award in the Arts (Media) in 2005. Vest, along with long-time journalist Michael Embry, founded *Kentucky Monthly* in 1998 and today it has a circulation of more than 40,000, with readers in every state and numerous foreign countries.

Steve is the author of two collections of his columns and the publisher of the anthology *Kentucky's Twelve Days of Christmas*. A native Kentuckian, Vest holds degrees from the University of Louisville (1986) and Murray State University (MFA in Creative Nonfiction, 2011). His work has appeared in literary journals such as Northern Kentucky University's *Journal of Kentucky Studies*, *Still*, *The Single Hound* (and others), as well as in the anthology, *Of Woods and Waters: An Outdoor Reader.*

Steve was a contributor to *The Encyclopedia of Northern Kentucky*. He is also the editor of *SAR Magazine*, the membership publication of the National Society, Sons of the American Revolution, which is based in Louisville, Kentucky.

Prior to starting *Kentucky Monthly*, Vest was the news editor of *The Blood-Horse*, an international Thoroughbred racing magazine based in Lexington, Kentucky. Before that, he spent more than a dozen years in newspapers, mostly in sports, including award-winning stints at the *Frankfort State*

Journal, the *Recorder Newspapers of Northern Kentucky* and the *McLean County News*.

Vest and his wife, Kay, reside in Frankfort with the youngest of their four delightful children.